PRAISE FOR *COURAG*

I can think of no one more qualified to speak to this topic than Beth Grant. She has spent her life bringing Jesus to some of the most exploited and abandoned people on the planet. I know she brings Jesus, not simply because of the words she says, but also because the love and compassion that flow from her heart are too deep, too sacrificial, and too unrelenting to be her own. You will get a glimpse of that love and compassion in these pages, but most of all, you will get a glimpse of Jesus.

Jeremy Vallerand, *President,*
Rescue: Freedom International

When I was living and working for a year as a researcher in Bangladesh in the early 1990s, I began to hear about Beth and David Grant. This couple, globally engaged and spiritually discerning, lived out the Great Commandment and the Great Commission. I saw it then. I see it now. Today, twenty years later, Dr. Beth Grant has given fresh perspective to the gospel at work in the lives of all of us ordinary working folks who can make a difference in our world for the cause of Christ. Her articulate and thoughtful presentation reflects her sharp mind and tender heart. But inside that tender heart is the courage of a warrior, rightly unsettled by the world's injustices. May the flames of the Spirit that burn deeply in Dr. Beth Grant's heart kindle anew the hearts of those who read this book.

Dr. Barry Corey, *President,*
Biola University, La Mirada, California

Courageous Compassion is a prophetic call to God's people for the twenty-first century. Your heart will burn, your mind will be challenged, and your vision expanded. Be aware—you will never be the same. God will speak to you, and you will discover new purpose for living, perhaps what He had in mind for you when you were born!

Dr. Jo Anne Lyon, *General Superintendent,*
The Wesleyan Church

Human trafficking and sexual exploitation of human beings has become a global pandemic. It now affects the lives of millions of women, men, boys, and girls in most countries of the world. Evangelical Christians are responding to this crisis through increased advocacy, direct intervention, public policy, and compassionate care. Beth Grant's *Courageous Compassion* is a call to action, prayer, and biblical transformation. Grant reminds us that social injustice is addressed throughout the Bible, and she challenges Christians to respond to this modern form of slavery. She advocates that we adopt a holistic and integrated compassion—one that seriously engages the human, social, and cultural realities of sexual exploitation and the work of God through Jesus Christ, who offers the ultimate answers to the problem of human pain. Writing as a practitioner, having spent years working globally to combat this evil, Beth takes us into the lives and stories of individuals who have experienced both painful abuse and God's redemptive grace. *Courageous Compassion* will serve churches, educators, activists, leaders, and others who seek to be better equipped in the fight against human trafficking.

Dr. Bill Prevette, *Oxford Centre for Missions Studies, Oxford, UK,*
Children and Youth at Risk—Research, Advocacy, and Intervention

Long before terms like *human trafficking, sexual slavery,* and *children-at-risk* were part of evangelical missiological discourse, David and Beth Grant were deeply immersed in compassionate and social justice issues. Beth Grant's *Courageous Compassion* draws from a two-decade repository of personal experiences in crafting this biblically sound yet powerfully engaging theology of social concern. In an age of unprecedented global social awareness, an emerging generation of restless Christ-followers, exposed to raw, gut-wrenching social realities on a daily basis, are increasingly discontented with pew-warming Christianity's cold response to such burning issues. Be warned . . . there is nothing cold or detached about this book. Grant is a thorough scholar, but unapologetically passionate in her attempt to draw her readers into a compelling and life-transforming journey that follows Jesus in courageous confrontation of social evil in our world. *Courageous Compassion* will appeal especially to readers, young and old, research scholar and grass-roots practitioner, whose concern with the question "Where would Jesus be and what would Jesus do if He were present in the flesh on planet earth today?" is not merely a matter of academic debate but a desire to know so they can go with Jesus, and follow Him in His healing mission to a broken world.

Dr. Ivan Satyavrata, *Senior Pastor,*
Assembly of God Mission, Kolkata, India

The passion that spills from every page of this book left me breathless with the implications of what Beth Grant has written. She and her husband, David, both ministers with the Assemblies of God, did not start a ministry: they saw a need and prayed until the Lord touched the heart of a national leader who would spearhead it. For the past seventeen years, they have encouraged the teams, helped raise money to fund Project Rescue, and have been prayer warriors themselves in this battle. Beth has shared her heart for trafficked women in many venues, and I am delighted that she has finally put it into print. The book is full of stories and practical suggestions for others to reflect and pray about as participants in the ministry. She tackles the American church's captivity to its culture in her discussion of the number of people who hear the need and decide on their own to do something about it without consulting or connecting with existing ministries. Working among the marginalized demands a level of trust that takes longer than a short-term mission trip to establish, and this book will challenge us in new ways to explore and take prayerful action against the evils of trafficking in our world.

Dr. Judith Lingenfelter, *Professor Emerita,*
Biola University, La Mirada, California

Courageous Compassion is a prophetic call to emulate Jesus—to meet the physical and spiritual needs of the poor and suffering. Beth Grant and her husband, David, have earned the right to speak on this subject. They have worked for many years around the world, rescuing women and children from sex-trafficking. They have seen firsthand what can be accomplished when Christ's followers administer compassion His way. This book is a clear and timely reminder that each one of us has a biblical duty to represent Jesus and His love. May it stir you beyond pity and sympathy to action.

Hal Donaldson, *President, Convoy of Hope*

During the decades I have known Beth and David Grant as colleagues and friends, they have consistently revealed their passion—not just any passion, but a passion for the Lord, the lost, and the Lord's work. The personal illustrations in the book are gripping and represent their hearts for ministering to hurting people. Their years of service in India and around the world have uniquely qualified them to share their theological perspective on compassion ministry and social justice. *Courageous Compassion: Confronting Social Injustice God's Way* is a resourceful and inspirational book that addresses one of the most important topics of this generation. I highly recommend reading it and using it in a group study environment to maximize discussion about our Pentecostal perspective on this vital and relevant issue.

Dr. Greg Mundis, *Executive Director, Assemblies of God World Missions*

Dr. Grant's book plumbs the depth and scope of compassion that is bold and courageous; a compassion that goes beyond mere words to translate those words into action. Grant admits that this kind of compassion is not only intricate but costly. To establish the validity of this claim, readers are taken on a heart-rending journey into the dark, tawdry arenas of the broken where life is lived in the context of evil and injustice. One's initial reaction is to recoil from the realities of the journey that reveals why only costly compassion will pierce through the deep darkness swirling around the broken, setting the captives free. However, since compassion exemplifies the character of God in who He is and how He responds to His children, the cost must be embraced. The journey also compels us to examine our own compassion. Is it adequate for transformative ministry, or do we find some gaping holes that need mending or replaced by the One called "the Father of all compassion?"

Dr. Phyllis Kilbourn, *Founder and Education Director,*
Crisis Care Training International

Courageous Compassion is a foundational work for understanding the complexities and challenges in combating human trafficking in the twenty-first century. Beth Grant has earned credentials in both the battlefield of anti-trafficking efforts around the world and the arena of research that strives for answers to one of the most insidious societal issues of our day. What she says is both strategic in reach and practical in application. The reader is invited to "figure things out and take action."

Within a biblical framework, Beth gives the reader reasons to keep reading and get involved in the battle. Her stories are current and true. Her suggestions are practical. And her passion for freeing the enslaved is felt on every page. It is not often that one finds a warrior who fights hard and writes well. Beth Grant is one of the few. Her book will challenge you to the core.

Dr. Dick Foth, *speaker,*
author of When the Giant Lies Down

From Mother Teresa's question: "What will you do today?" to the question from a madam regarding a girl who was no longer desired: "Do you want her?", *Courageous Compassion* challenges you to do much more than simply learn about caring for others. Warning: this book is best read with a box of tissues! The stories of astounding human need are gut-wrenching and gripping. The heart-stirring testimonies of triumphant victories won through simple acts of compassion will motivate you to courageous and compassionate action!

Rod Loy, *Senior Pastor,*
First Assembly of God, North Little Rock Arkansas;
author of Three Questions *and* Immediate Obedience

Across church history, the pendulum of truth about proclamation, an emphasis on evangelism, and a primary focus on good works has swung from one extreme to another. For example, at times all emphasis has been on proclamation, with little focus on the church's call to feed the hungry and break the bonds of the oppressed. At other times the Word of God is downplayed in favor of deeds. This swinging pendulum is a topic of special relevance today. We are blessed with a generation of young people who want to be involved in what God is doing and are seeking His direction. If we look to Scripture, we find clarity in Acts 6, when the disciples were confronted with a similar challenge. After prayer and direction from the Holy Spirit, they set the pattern, saying, "It is not reasonable for us to leave the preaching of the gospel, and wait on tables." Right here is set once and for all the priority of the church. That priority is proclamation—the reality that the soul is more important than the body, and eternity is more important than time. However, the early church also took deliberate action to meet the challenge of feeding the hungry and caring for the poor. They organized a plan so the poor would not be neglected—an important part of the church's mission.

In *Courageous Compassion*, Beth Grant presents a sound biblical position of ministering to spiritual needs, while giving a cup of cold water in the name of Jesus. We are to live our lives with balance, both proclaiming the truth that there is no other name whereby men must be saved, while also walking out that truth by doing good works, if need be, to sacrifice ourselves to accomplish this. I commend the message of the book and am grateful that Beth used her great gifts and talents in the area of missiology and writing to share this message.

Bob Hoskins, *Founder, OneHope*

I have known Beth Grant as a colleague and friend for many years. In all of that time, I have never seen her passion to fight against human trafficking wane or waiver. Instead, she has shared that passion through her writing, teaching, speaking, and personal example, challenging all of us to consider how God would use us to do "something" about this tragedy of human suffering. In *Courageous Compassion*, Dr. Grant lays a solid biblical foundation for informed compassion outreach. She demonstrates the mandate for Christian response, pointing to scriptures that give us direction for "best practice" in our approach to anti-trafficking interventions. She beautifully portrays the need to trust God, cast fear aside, while encouraging us to work together, to join hands with the local church and those who know the culture and context of a particular setting. This is a must-read for every Christian and certainly for anyone wishing to begin an anti-trafficking outreach.

JoAnn Butrin, *PhD, Director of International Ministries, Assemblies of God World Missions*

Beth Grant goes beyond challenging the church in *Courageous Compassion*. She shares a prophetic word to the church. Our private and public responses to the injustices in the world must be met with the posture of compassion modeled by our Savior. The book is replete with gripping personal story lines and substantiated with adroit analysis. Every university student needs to give *Courageous Compassion* a read.

E. Scott and Crystal Martin, *National Directors, Chi Alpha Campus Ministry*

Once the church is established, it must courageously and compassionately represent the full-orbed rule of Christ (kingdom) in every aspect of society. The church stands for justice and righteousness and against evil wherever it is found. In mission therefore, there is a logical priority on planting churches among unreached peoples and an undeniable responsibility for the planted church to be compassionate. Dr. Beth Grant both lives and articulates the harmony of these complementary and inseparable passions of God. We must plant the church where it does not exist, and that church must display God's sacrificial and practical love to the world. *Courageous Compassion* resists being consumed with treating symptoms and lovingly works towards the long-range cure of God.

Dick Brogden, *Live Dead Arab World, Cairo, Egypt*

In *Courageous Compassion*, Beth Grant provides a substantive overview of a framework for compassion that demonstrates faith and action, and is nothing short of world changing. Her most profound challenge to the local church compassion ministry is also often the most problematic, the untapped power of collaboration. Her call to reflect, review, and revise our old patterns of independence, and work to build a collaborative model of justice, is supported by hard won lessons and counsel. I believe that this will not only transform the world, it will transform the church, and, it will transform us.

Dr. Sandie Morgan, *Director, Center for Women's Studies, and Founder of Live2Free, Vanguard University*

We live in a culture that engages life mind-first. Greed is called industry, covetousness is called ambition, and hoarding, prudence. This book is a clarion call of the apostle Paul's exhortation to be renewed in the spirit of our minds (Eph. 4:23). It is a reminder that we ought to have a heart-first and compassionate mind-set, hence an integrated transformational approach to compassion and justice desperately needed today.

Dr. Jesse Miranda, *President and Founder, The Jesse Miranda Center for Hispanic Leadership, Vanguard University*

COURAGEOUS
C O M P A S S I O N

CONFRONTING SOCIAL INJUSTICE

GOD'S WAY

BETH GRANT

MY HEALTHY CHURCH

Cover design by Sheepish Design www.sheepishdesign.org

Interior formatting by Prodigy Pixel www.prodigypixel.com

NOTE: Some of the names in this book, as well as some identifying details, have been changed to protect the anonymity of the people involved.

CONTENTS

ACKNOWLEDGEMENTS

Courageous Compassion has come into being because of dear family, friends, and colleagues who have modeled courageous compassion for Christ's mission among the hurting wherever God has placed them in His world.

- My husband, David, the most generous compassionate visionary I have ever known

- Our daughters, Rebecca Shults and Jennifer Barratt, who lived the journey with us

- Our sons-in-law, Jonathan Barratt and Tyler Shults, who had no idea what they were getting into, but have embraced this journey with all their hearts and God-given strengths

- Rev. Drs. Mark and Huldah Buntain, founders of AG Mission, Calcutta with all its compassionate outreach

- Rev. David Mohan, All-India General Superintendent of the Assemblies of God, Chennai, New Life founder and pastor

- Dr. George O. Wood, General Superintendent of The General Council of the Assemblies of God, USA

- K. K. Devaraj and Latijah, founder and director of Bombay Teen Challenge, Mumbai, India

- Rev. Ambika Pandey, founder and director of Deepika Welfare Society, Kolkata, India

- Dr. John and Faith Higgins, pastor and director of Assemblies of God Mission, Kolkata, India
- Dr. Ivan and Sheila Satyavrata, Pastor of Assemblies of God Mission, Kolkata, and Chairman of the Board, Deepika Welfare Society, Kolkata
- Doug and Ramona Jacobs, founders of Project Rescue Nepal
- Easo and Leela Daniel, Project Rescue Sharansthan, Nagpur, India
- Mathew and Suha Daniel, founders of Project Rescue Pune, India
- Pastor Gavin and Amenla Cunningham, First Assembly of God, Bangalore, India
- Joni Middleton, Project Rescue trainer and program consultant for children
- Andy and Nancy Raatz, AGWM, founders of Freedom Home, Moldova
- Pastor Robert Jeyaraj, Global Christian Life Church, Delhi, India
- Rohit and Vinita Bhalla, founders of Suraksha Project Rescue Delhi, India
- Kevin and Lucy Donaldson, Project Rescue Delhi, India
- George Varghese, Project Rescue Foundation India
- Sumi Samuel and Arul Santosh, directors of Project Rescue, New Life AG, Chennai, India

- Pastor Rajnish and Oriana Jacob, Jaipur, India, founder of ministry to Rajasthani villages of generational prostitution

- Fiona Bellshaw, founder and director of Project Rescue, Madrid, Spain

- Angela Trementozzi, Europe, Assemblies of God World Missions

- Lisa Russi, founder of Project Rescue Bangladesh

- Mel and Jillian Rogers, Project Rescue, Bangladesh

- Dr. JoAnn Butrin, Director of International Ministries AGWM, compassion ministries specialist

- Cindy Hudlin, AGWM colleague and co-editor and project manager of *Hands That Heal*

- Lisa Thompson, formerly anti-trafficking specialist Salvation Army World Office, now World Hope coordinator of anti-trafficking

- Dr. Joann Lyon, Wesleyan Methodist Church General Superintendent, former CEO of World Hope

- Dr. Sandie Morgan, Vanguard University Center for Women's Studies, founder of Live2Free, former director of Southern California Orange County Anti-Trafficking Task Force

- Dr. Melody Palm, director of counseling, Assemblies of God Theological Seminary and trauma counseling specialist for the sexually abused

- Patricia Green, pioneer of ministry to prostituted women in Bangkok, Thailand, founder and director of Alabaster Box, Berlin, Germany
- Lauran Bethell, pioneer of ministries to prostituted women in Asia and Europe, international consultant and trainer

INTRODUCTION

A PERSONAL FRAMEWORK FOR COMPASSION MINISTRIES

Compassion ministry is not something I recall as a topic of my life and upbringing in a small Pentecostal church in the suburbs of Washington, DC. I grew up in a Christian family where compassion was routinely practiced as a part of my parents' personal faith journey. More than once, I recall needy strangers showing up on our doorstep because my father, who never knew a stranger, had invited them to come to our home. My mother was the planner and organizer, so her compassionate responses were always more well-planned, reflective, and deliberate. But from both of my parents' examples, sharing the cup of cold water (Matt. 10:42) was a natural-as-breathing part of following Jesus.

Then my missionary-evangelist husband, David, took me to India in 1977. A week after we were married, he proudly took his new bride, previously widowed at twenty-five, to meet the people and nation he loved so passionately. And suddenly the word *compassion* exploded into my formerly orderly world. In a context of staggering human need I couldn't have imagined before, my inobtrusive definition of compassion was challenged with the "storm-the-gates-of-hell" activism of missionary evangelist Mark Buntain. I watched him feed the hungry, weep over alcoholics, start a hospital, and take in hurting children—all between Sundays of powerfully preaching the Word, when the broken in Kolkata heard the booming voice of the evangelist and prophet calling them to Jesus. And they came.

And so did the missiological debates on compassion ministries. I began to hear terms like *social gospel* spoken in hushed voices. I sat on some of my first Assemblies of God World Missions committees, where we had to avoid using the word *holistic*. I participated in discussions where proclamation and compassion were viewed as competing missions. During those years, my graduate studies provided a gift of reflection on the life of Christ and missiology interspersed between times of immersion in the sense-assaulting needs of Kolkata, Mumbai, and Delhi. My husband, David, continued to preach Jesus and missions, and responded compassionately to the overwhelming human needs.

Then came our colleague K. K. Devaraj's first visit to Mumbai's Kamatapura red-light district in 1996. He and his wife, Latijah, had moved to Mumbai to pioneer a Teen Challenge ministry among the city's young men on the streets, but for the first time God led Devaraj to take his outreach team into a place the church rarely goes. Kamatapura opened our eyes to a world of horrendous sexual exploitation among tens of thousands of victimized women and children—a world we had never known existed. When trafficked Nepali women told the Teen Challenge team they wanted to follow Jesus but couldn't leave the brothels where they were enslaved, they asked Devaraj to take their young daughters to safety. He called my husband, David, in the middle of the night and tearfully asked a question that changed the course of our lives and ministry: *"Brother Grant, can we take thirty-seven little girls?"*

Without a thought of how, where, or whether this fit with our missiology, my husband responded with a resounding, "Of course we can!" The vision for Project Rescue—a ministry to sexually-enslaved women and children in Eurasia—was born. It was also the beginning of my personal journey to understand how this fit with our larger Matthew 28:19 mission. Nothing in all our prior years of ministry had evoked the depth of human emotion that the needs of the sexually-exploited did, both in our team and our partners. I felt personally responsible to make sure we stayed in the center of God's redemptive stream and were not distracted by the immensity of this need and the unprecedented emotional response to it.

The months and years that followed, as God has grown Project Rescue ministries, have been challenging and inspiring, liberating and frustrating, formidable and amazing. We've been encouraged and discouraged, helped and hindered, admired and mistrusted . . . sometimes all in the same day! Our mission leadership, perplexed at times by our direction, have received doubt-filled calls from pastors asking disarming questions such as, "David Grant is doing *what* with prostitutes?"

But on this journey, we've come to know, as never before, an unconditionally compassionate God and His power to save and transform the lives of the enslaved. We've seen His grace at work in thousands of complicated lives that had never known grace before. We've made mistakes, and we've had to learn as we tried to obey the guidance of His Spirit. As we and our team members have continued to share the hope of new life in Jesus Christ with the most broken, God has continued to change lives.

We've learned some liberating hands-on lessons about our biblical mission:

- We can call upon Jesus and His name in a brothel, and He hears and answers prayer.

- Every woman and every little girl has been created by God and given life for a purpose—a good purpose. Each was created to become a woman of God.

- Spiritual darkness is more than a concept. It's a smothering, tangible, destructive reality.

- Spiritual light is more than a concept. Jesus is a liberating, loving, healing, transforming reality!

- There is no place so dark that the light of Jesus cannot shine.

- Jesus-like compassion is not anemic, pale, and nonconfrontational. It's bold, necessarily courageous, and disruptively life-changing.

In the pages that follow, you will find stories of the sexually enslaved who found freedom, as well as those of ministry colleagues who walked the life-changing and sometimes painful journey with them. Much of what you will read is distilled from years of passionate investment into my students' lives as intercultural ministers, and their contribution back to me as their teacher and co-learner. I sincerely hope that you will prayerfully consider the truths and principles embedded here and will share them with others in your family, church, and classes. Together we can explore Jesus' Luke 4 mandate in our twenty-first-century world: *The Spirit of the Lord is on me, because he has anointed me to proclaim good news to the poor. He has sent me to proclaim freedom for the prisoners and recovery of sight for the blind, to set the oppressed free, to proclaim the year of the Lord's favor (Luke 4:18–19).*

CHAPTER 1

WHEN GOD STOOD UP: AN ISAIAH 59 COMPASSION

So justice is far from us, and righteousness does not reach us.
We look for light, but all is darkness; for
brightness, but we walk in deep shadows.
Like the blind we grope along the wall, feeling
our way like people without eyes.
At midday we stumble as if it were twilight;
among the strong, we are like the dead . . .
We look for justice, but find none; for
deliverance, but it is far away.
For our offenses are many in your sight,
and our sins testify against us.
Our offenses are ever with us, and we acknowledge our iniquities:
Rebellion and treachery against the LORD,
turning our backs on our God,
Inciting revolt and oppression, uttering
lies our hearts have conceived.
So justice is driven back, and righteousness stands at a distance;
Truth has stumbled in the streets, honesty cannot enter.
Truth is nowhere to be found, and whoever shuns evil
becomes a prey.

ISAIAH 59:9–15A

n September of 2010, I first heard news of a tragic twenty-first-century story of injustice that is becoming far too common. A young woman of twenty-one had been admitted to a local hospital emergency room in cardiac arrest. As the medical first responders provided urgent care to the patient, they realized something was horribly wrong. She showed visible signs of torture and violent sexual abuse. In the days that followed, the sickening story unfolded.

At fifteen, the mentally-challenged victim had been offered a place to live with a man and woman in their home. The teenage girl, looking for help, instead found herself in physical and sexual slavery for the next five years. She underwent barbaric sexual torture and rape, all to be captured for paying "customers" who had an appetite for cruelty and sexual perversion either as participants, observers, or consumers of video pornography. The captive young woman, who had gone into cardiac arrest because of the severe trauma, was finally freed from her captors and placed into care. Ironically, her perpetrators tried to defend their actions by saying the young woman enjoyed her abuse and liked posing for pornography. Twenty-first-century "truth" in an Isaiah 59 world. [1]

The prophet Isaiah's description of the context of evil and injustice is compelling for the contemporary Christian on several levels. First, the passage is graphically dark, evil, and hopeless in content and eerily descriptive of many global cities today. The writer could easily be describing dark areas of Mumbai, Cairo, Moscow, Johannesburg, or Mexico City, that are gripped by exploitation and violence. Or, as in the case of the news story

---

1   "Springfield Man, Four Others Indicted in Sex Conspiracy," *Springfield News-Leader,* September 10, 2010: B1.

above, it sadly also depicts small towns in southwest Missouri. The scope is different in rural America, but the tone of tangible evil, its manifested violence, and its effect on victims are just the same. When over a quarter of a million children and youth in the United States are victimized in commercial sexual exploitation each year,[2] global injustice has come home.

The unrestrained evil of greed and injustice, so effectively pictured by Isaiah, reminds us of the tragic faces of "dead" girls walking in red-light districts around the world. In the prophet's words, ". . . among the strong, we are like the dead" (Isa. 59:10a). While the dress and demeanor of sexual slavery differ from culture to culture, the eyes do not lie; they are tragically the same the world over. The effect of this extreme darkness and its accompanying sexual violence is the emotional, spiritual, and psychological death of the victims, which leaves them as empty physical shells in place of once-vibrant, innocent girls. Just as God created women and children to worship Him with body, mind, and spirit, evil injustice destroys body, mind, and spirit—creating seemingly hopeless shame that separates its victims from God. Their bodies must continue to perform as demanded through intimidation and control day after day, but deadened eyes give heartbreaking witness to the inner death of the person.

---

2   Luke Gilkerson, "$28-Billion-Crime: New film shows the dark connection between sex addiction and sex trafficking." *Covenant Eyes*. http://www.covenanteyes.com/pureminds-articles/28-billion-crime-new-film-shows-the-dark-connection-between-sex-addiction-and-sex-trafficking/.

THE REALITY OF A COMPASSIONATE
GOD WHO LOVES JUSTICE

But thankfully, Isaiah 59 does not end with verse 15!

> The LORD looked and was displeased that there was
> no justice.
> He saw that there was no one, he was appalled that
> there was no one to intervene;
> so his own arm achieved salvation for him, and his
> own righteousness sustained him.
> He put on righteousness as his breastplate, and the
> helmet of salvation on his head;
> He put on garments of vengeance and wrapped
> himself in zeal as in a cloak.
> According to what they have done, so will he repay
> wrath to his enemies and retribution to his foes; he will
> repay the islands their due.
> From the west, men will fear the name of the LORD,
> and from the rising of the sun, they will revere his glory.
> (Isaiah 59:16–19a)

In the face of twenty-first-century darkness, violence, and injustice, the prophet's message wonderfully illuminates truth about the God we serve:

1. God is not impervious, untouched, or unfeeling
   about the past, present, or future state of injustice
   and its effects. While being "appalled" is not a
   quality we generally ascribe to God, Isaiah indicates

"God was appalled" that there was no one to help and intervene.

2. God is not intimidated by spiritual darkness. Rather, He stood up to it in time and place by sending Jesus, His Son. Through Jesus, God intervened with truth, righteousness, and redemption.

3. God's compassionate response was and is bold, courageous, and epic! There is nothing tentative, hesitant, or hand-wringing about the tone or words of our Father's response to the violence and injustice Isaiah describes.

But as in all of Scripture, the reality of the darkness in Isaiah 59 and God's response to it demands a response from His children. God was and is appalled. Are we? Where is the church—God's people—in the face of great spiritual darkness, violence, and injustice? Are we

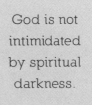

God is not intimidated by spiritual darkness.

wringing our proverbial hands? Are we declining to comment? Have we lost our God-given voice? Or are we responding in the spirit and example of Jesus, whom we follow? These are the questions the Holy Spirit is asking us as followers of Jesus and members of the community of faith. These are the kinds of unsettling prophetic questions that demand deep soul-searching and have inspired this call to action. In the face of great darkness and evil, it's time for God's people to stand up!

A COURAGEOUS COMPASSION

But how can we move from a tentative, anemic compassion to a bold, courageous one? What steps can we take?

1. STUDY THE LIFE OF JESUS THROUGH THE LENS OF HIS COMPASSIONATE RESPONSES TO PEOPLE IN NEED. HE IS OUR ULTIMATE MODEL.

Exploring the life of Jesus in the Gospels, several patterns emerge in His compassionate responses that would have been seen as bold and unusual in His cultural and historical context. The people He helped were often marginalized by society: children, women, the physically disabled, and the demonized, along with a few scoundrels!

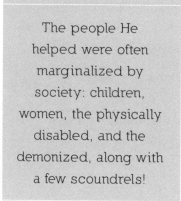

> The people He helped were often marginalized by society: children, women, the physically disabled, and the demonized, along with a few scoundrels!

It's not insignificant that those who drew Jesus' attention two thousand years ago still represent huge segments of our world's population today. Not infrequently, they still remain devalued, stigmatized, and/or exploited in culture after culture.

If we consider only one of the groups Jesus related to with compassion—children—and view them with His eyes in contemporary world issues, the result is revealing. In the twenty-first century, of the 2.2 billion children in the world, 1.5 billion—two-thirds!—are children at risk or in crisis.[3]

---

3   Phyllis Kilbourn, *Healing for Hurting Hearts: A Handbook for Counseling Children and Youth in Crisis* (Fort Washington, PA: CLC Publications, 2013).

Children are frequently the most victimized in nation after nation where evil reigns:[4]

- Children pressed to become soldiers in ethnic conflicts
- Children victimized by sexual abuse and incest in dysfunctional families
- Children sold for prostitution
- Children forced into child labor where poverty abounds
- Children offered to idols in religious rituals where demonic power is engaged
- Children used as commodities in arranged child marriages
- Children traded as commodities in sex tourism for pedophiles
- Children groomed for child pornography through internet chat rooms

And tragically, the list goes on! But the actions and words of Jesus in Luke's gospel stand out in prophetic contrast:

---

4   See Dr. Phyllis Kilbourn's curricula focusing on ministry to specific groups of vic-
     timized children worldwide. Crisis Care Training International, "About Curriculum,"
     http://crisiscaretraining.org/about-crisis-care-training/about-curriculum/. See also
     Rainbows of Hope, "Resources," http://rainbowsofhope.org/resourceswp.

But Jesus called the children to him and said, "Let the little children come to me, and do not hinder them, for the kingdom of God belongs to such as these." (Luke 18:16)

And afterwards, Jesus took the children in his arms and placed His hands of blessing on them (Mark 10:16). As the contemporary church, what are we doing to bless the children in our local community as Jesus blessed them?

One of the greatest ways we can bless children in our local community and around the world is not only to bless them physically, emotionally, and spiritually in Jesus' name, but to train them to practice compassion and bless others in the same way. God blesses His children with opportunities to be a source of His blessing and compassion to others. While the church easily grasps that privilege for adults, it's easy for us to be negligent in enabling, training, and empowering children who love Jesus to do the same. This valuing of children with spiritual responsibility is radical in traditional cultures. But Scripture reveals the Creator God of heaven and earth, who is above all kingdoms, principalities, and powers, blesses children to bless others.[5]

> Some of the most powerful prayers that have ever been prayed over David and me have been prayed by little girls in Mumbai, India, who were born into brothels.

---

5   Douglas McConnell, Jennifer Orona, and Paul Stockley, eds., *Understanding God's Heart for Children: Toward a Biblical Framework* (USA: Authentic Media, 2007).

To illustrate, some of the most powerful prayers that have ever been prayed over David and me have been prayed by little girls in Mumbai, India, who were born into brothels. These little ones who have come out of such great Isaiah 59 darkness and evil, and who have seen horror I can't even imagine, have been taught by their spiritual caregivers that they, too, can call on God in Jesus' name, and He will hear and answer their prayers.

"Auntie, can we pray for you?" I was humbled and amazed by that question from a frail little girl whose mother is stigmatized by society as one of "those women."

"Of course! I would love for you to pray for me!" As I knelt on the floor in humility, little girls of five, six, and seven surrounded me—little girls who now knew Jesus and began to pray faith-filled prayers, disarming in their sincerity and simplicity.

"Jesus, you know I am just a little girl and this is a great woman of God." (By now, I am utterly humbled.) "But Jesus, I know you hear my prayers. Please bless this Auntie! In Jesus' name. Amen."

Courageous compassion has many faces around our globe. But it takes a bold compassion—like the compassion of Jesus—to bless, restore, and empower those whom the powerful of this world view as weak and unimportant. Through the eyes of Jesus, we see those to whom He was drawn as He did: potential men and women of God on a healing, life-changing journey.

2. INTENTIONALLY CULTIVATE, THROUGH PRAYER AND BIBLE STUDY, A GROWING AWARENESS OF THE BELIEVER'S SPIRITUAL AND MORAL AUTHORITY IN JESUS AND ITS ACCOMPANYING COMPASSIONATE RESPONSIBILITY TO THOSE AROUND US.

Several years before Mother Teresa's death, our daughters and I had the opportunity to visit her in the Mother's House in Kolkata. One of the first things that struck me about this unassuming but highly respected woman was that such strength and courage were housed in a woman no larger than our twelve-year-old daughter, Jennifer. There was tangible humility and apparent sacrifice, yet great authority.

A wealthy businessman from Kolkata had arranged an appointment with Mother Teresa just before ours. She invited us to sit with them as they met. Quickly it became clear that the businessman had come for Mother's blessing on him, his family, and his prospering textile business. But as he complimented her profusely and began to implore her for a blessing, Mother Teresa interrupted him: "But what will you do for my poor?"

This man of authority was visibly taken aback and attempted again to ask for Mother's blessing. Again, she cut him off and said with boldness, "But what will you do for my poor?" The businessman was obviously uncomfortable and began to try to explain how much he had already done by donating sari material for the poor. Yet again, Mother Teresa was not deterred.

"That is good. But what will you do *today*?"

This diminutive woman's boldness was remarkable. In pondering that exchange many times since, I've realized that she could be so daringly bold to ask because she was genuinely asking for the poor, not for herself. Part of her spiritual commitment was a vow to poverty, which she and her sisters kept faithfully. Thus her concern and action on behalf of the poor and dying of Kolkata had integrity and ethical authority, as they were based on and lived out from Jesus' compassion for the poor. Her compassionate initiatives

were not self-serving, but about
"her poor" for whom she sacrificially
worked and lived.

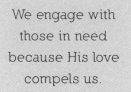

We engage with
those in need
because His love
compels us.

Clearly, most of us are not
called to the same life and ministry
as Mother Teresa. However, we can
learn from the bold compassion she
lived out and articulated on a daily basis. It was Jesus-focused, Jesus-initiated, and Jesus-impassioned. Her life conveyed a compassion of moral and ethical authority that captivated everyone—the poor and the rich; Hindus, Muslims, and Christians; the smallest child and the greatest statesman.

Twenty-first century followers of Jesus who practice compassion, whatever our profession, must monitor our motivations and guard our hearts and minds. Sadly, the spiritual and ethical authority of the church and people of faith are undermined when so-called compassion ministries become driven by personal ambition and profit. Christ-like compassion is a natural-as-breathing outcome of walking close enough to Jesus on a day-to-day basis that we catch His Father's heart. We weep over those for whom He weeps. We engage with those in need because His love compels us.

3. COURAGEOUS COMPASSION DEMANDS THAT WE COME TO TERMS WITH OUR FEARS.

Besides powerfully exposing God's response to a world of injustice, the prophet Isaiah's description in chapter 59 reminds us that injustice, violence, slavery, and evil in all their forms have contexts. They are not mere concepts or social issues that occur in physical, emotional, and spiritual vacuums. While issue-focused conferences are excellent, they can sometimes dull the reality and significance of context in understanding and practicing life-changing compassion. HIV/AIDS, poverty, rape as a weapon of war, homelessness, substance abuse, population displacement, domestic violence, sex trafficking, and every other social evil and ill one can name all take place in real places with challenging and complex dynamics. And perhaps that is what we fear the most: danger, violence, perversion, hatred, greed, anger, hostility, fear, betrayal, rebellion, murder, intimidation, lies, fighting, disease, treachery, anarchy, and even death.

As twenty-first-century Christians, we would be Good Samaritans—if only those beaten and robbed and left to die weren't on the most dangerous, isolated roads in our cities. We would gladly bring Christ's hope to the "Mary Magdalenes" of our world—if they didn't hang out in red-light districts with men in sexual bondage. We would pray prayers of deliverance for demoniacs—if they just weren't quite so violent and unpredictable. Yes, they would all be welcome in our churches . . . if only.

But there is good news! Leader Jack Hayford states, "There is a huge awakening for social concern today,"[6] and notes that this isn't a new phenomenon for Pentecostals. Many of Christ's followers are stirred, not only by the pressing needs in our spiritually dark world, but by the empowering Holy Spirit, who dispels fear and gives His children a holy boldness to act.[7] Many of God's people around the world are standing up, and chains of fear are being broken by the One who has the power to cast out all fear (1 John 4:15–19). In the pages to come, we will catch glimpses of some of their inspiring stories, and of God's life-changing justice and compassion.

---

6   Quoted by Robert C. Crosby in "A New Kind of Pentecostal," *Christianity Today*, August 3, 2011, http://www.christianitytoday.com/ct/2011/august/newkindpentecostal.html.

7   See chapter 12, "Supernatural Power for a Supernatural Compassion," page 247.

QUESTIONS FOR COMPASSIONATE ENGAGEMENT

1. How does my view of compassion ministry compare or contrast with the Isaiah 59 view presented in this chapter?

2. When confronted with reports of violence, sexual abuse and injustice in my local community, what is my inner, private response? What is my public response?

3. What influences shape and define my response to injustice the most? How and why?

4. When our local church is confronted with reports of violence, sexual abuse, and injustice in our community, what is the response?

5. As we prayerfully look at our own situations, what is God asking us as individuals, as families, and as a church to do to stand up and bring God's love and power to the darkest places in our world—to those who are enslaved in great darkness?

6. Prayerfully consider what might be the first steps that God would have you take in order to obey Him in courageous compassion. Finish the sentence, "I would do _____, if only _____." Using God's Word for guidance, what is His response?

SUGGESTED LEARNING EXPERIENCE

In a small group, begin to research and pray about the most pressing needs in your city or community. Identify people and issues that would be of most concern to those in leadership in your city.

Prayerfully consider what you as individuals and as the community of faith could do to help meet that need. Identify and pray about the hindrances—including fears—that might prevent acts of courageous compassion. Plan action steps to take compassionate, Spirit-led engagement in your community to a new level.

FOR FURTHER STUDY

- Crosby, Robert C. "A New Kind of Pentecostal." *Christianity Today,* August 3, 2011.

- Kilbourn, Phyllis, ed. *Shaping the Future: Girls and Our Destiny.* Pasadena, CA: William Carey Library, 2008.

- McConnell, Douglas, Jennifer Orona, and Paul Shockley, eds. *Understanding God's Heart for Children: Toward a Biblical Framework.* Colorado Springs, CO: Authentic Publishing, 2007.

- Miles, Glenn, and Josephine-Joy Wright, eds. *Celebrating Children: Equipping People Working with Children and Young People Living in Difficult Circumstances Around the World.* Oxford: Paternoster Biblical and Theological Monographs, 2004.

CHAPTER 2

A CALL FOR AN
INTEGRATED COMPASSION

This is how we know what love is: Jesus
Christ laid down his life for us.
And we ought to lay down our lives for our brothers and sisters.
If anyone has material possessions and sees a
brother or sister in need but has no pity on them,
how can the love of God be in that person?
Dear children, let us not love with words or
speech, but with actions and in truth.
1 JOHN 3:16–18

Excitement was in the air on a hot afternoon at Ashagram, City of Hope. All the women and children who had come out of the red-light district to find new life, along with the young men in the Bombay Teen Challenge program, were gathered with staff and guests for an enthusiastic day of celebration. It was time for the graduates of the BTC ministry community to receive their diplomas and to recognize their achievement in completing the discipleship training program.

Then it came time to honor the women who had come out of modern-day slavery and found new life and healing through Christ Jesus. It was a deeply emotional moment as ladies in beautiful new saris walked shyly across the platform to receive their diplomas. For most of them, this would be the first time in their lives to be honored and recognized for accomplishing something of value. That fact alone is difficult to grasp for those of us who have been honored from kindergarten with various kinds of awards.

One woman in particular caught my eye and heart. She was dressed in a vibrant purple sari. As she approached me with tentative steps to receive her diploma and a prayer of blessing, there were tears flowing over a face visibly scarred by the years of violence. But the joy and grace covering this woman were riveting. With humility and lowered eyes she received the diploma and prayers as the BTC community, from oldest to youngest, cheered and clapped.

> Jesus' practice of compassion was a natural, integral part of His earthly mission of redemption—not a separate initiative.

As we left the celebration, K. K. Devaraj asked if I had noticed the woman in purple. He went on to remind me of the night that a madam in Kamatapura had called him. One of "her women" had totally disintegrated, mentally and emotionally, and was running without clothes through the district. This woman was worthless to her now. Did Devaraj want her? Immediately, the minister and his outreach team headed for the red-light district, where they hunted and found the traumatized woman, wrapped her in blankets, and took her to Ashagram. There, in an environment of Jesus-like compassion, prayer, the Word, and patient Spirit-led counseling, the woman began the healing journey. This was the woman in the purple sari.

JESUS' MODEL OF INTEGRATED COMPASSION

A study of Christ's life reveals a captivating image of compassion. As His followers, we can learn from the compassion He modeled:

- *Jesus fed* the hungry (Matt. 15:29–39)
- *Jesus reached* to bring the son back to life (Luke 7:11–14)
- *Jesus touched and healed* the man with leprosy (Luke 5:12–13)
- *Jesus walked in spiritual authority* to deliver two men of demon possession (Matt. 8:28–32)
- *Jesus wept* at the death of his friend Lazarus (John 11:33–39)
- *Jesus spoke truth* to one with whom the religious would not speak—the woman at the well (John 4:7, 26)
- *Jesus released those in spiritual, mental, and emotional slavery*—the demon-possessed son (Luke 9:37–43)

What is significant for this study on compassion is that the larger picture of Jesus' earthly ministry shows how He lived out His Father's mission: teaching, healing, touching, weeping, speaking, releasing, feeding, and preaching, all in integrated moment-by-moment obedience to His Father. Jesus' practice of compassion was a natural, integral part of His earthly mission of redemption—not a separate initiative. While Jesus used His disciples as a part of His "outreach," as when He fed the four thousand, the feeding flowed out of His concern for the needs of people He loved, had come to save, and wanted to teach.

This may appear rather obvious and elementary as we explore the life of Christ; however, it's significant as many in the Western church tend to dichotomize the role of preaching and teaching from compassion.[8] Compassion ministries are seen as separate from evangelism and discipleship. In contrast, much of the global church in the two-thirds world does not distinguish compassion ministries in this way, but views them as a natural, integral part of the gospel and the church's fulfillment of the Great Commission. This historical tendency of our Western worldview to dichotomize these aspects of Christian ministry drove us to carefully evaluate Project Rescue's mission from the beginning. We determined to evaluate how it fit integrally—if indeed it did—into the larger mission of our parent organization. That process of assessing and safeguarding our mission to ensure it fit squarely in word and practice into the whole of our denomination's mission drove us back to revisit God's Word and our missiology. A fierce determination to make sure our compassionate actions were grounded in Christ, His life, and mission became the foundation for this book and continues to this day.

The following model illustrates an assessment process for specific compassionate initiatives, their mission, and their integration with the whole of a church's or ministry's fulfillment of the Great Commission. The specific model is taken from the Assemblies of God World Mission's strategic model at the time Project Rescue began, and includes our description of how the affiliated ministries fit within it. The ministry's mission is "to rescue and restore victims of

---

8   An excellent debate on this Western dichotomous view and its effect on mission is found in "The Bad Question of Proclamation vs. Social Action: A Symposium," *Evangelical Missions Quarterly* 48, no. 3 (July 2012): 264–271.

sexual slavery through the love and power of Jesus Christ." Our goal
is an integrated biblical compassion that brings healing to the whole
person—body, mind, and spirit—wherever intervention occurs.

REACHING Evangelism	PLANTING Faith Communities	TRAINING Discipleship	TOUCHING Compassion
Red-light district outreaches	Red-light district church	Vocational training centers	Medical clinics & HIV/AIDS testing
Red-light district Sunday schools	Vocational training center	Aftercare homes	Education of children in programs
Vocational training center	Integration of women, children into local faith communities	Red-light district church & Sunday schools	After-school programs & night-care shelter
Medical clinic in red-light district		After-school programs in RLD	Aftercare homes

The model is helpful for minister practitioners involved in
compassion ministries to visualize several key truths.

1. IN ORDER TO BE BIBLICALLY LIFE-CHANGING,
COMPASSION MINISTRIES MUST BE INTEGRATED
WITH ALL ASPECTS OF JESUS' GREAT COMMISSION
OR EVANGELISM OUTREACH AND DISCIPLESHIP IN
CONTEXTUALIZED FORMS (MATT. 28:19–20).

Sharing Jesus' hope in a brothel or a Starbucks coffee shop doesn't
look the same as sharing it in a conference, concert, or church.

However, sharing His love is at the heart of the gospel and of biblical compassion ministry—and can happen naturally anywhere, at any moment. The same is true of discipleship, which can be formal or informal. What is critical is that they are intentionally, naturally, and consistently at the heart of our compassionate engagement.

Importantly, help is extended by our Project Rescue-affiliated colleagues to all women and children in local areas of prostitution who want help, regardless of their religious background. They are working in Hindu, Muslim, Orthodox, and Catholic nations. However, the programs all include the basic disciplines of our faith as followers of Jesus: prayer, devotions, worship, and discipleship. Participation in each program is a choice where all are welcome.

2. THE SPIRITUAL AND MISSIONAL STRENGTH OF COMPASSION MINISTRIES DEPEND ON INTERACTION WITH A LOCAL COMMUNITY OF FAITH, THE CHURCH.

Where else but in the local community of faith can we find the necessary intercession, Christian staff, volunteers, resources, accountability, and community required for a life-changing initiative? (See chapter 8, "The Catalyst of Community")

3. INTENTIONALITY AND COMMITMENT TO MISSION ARE KEYS TO LIFE-CHANGING COMPASSION AND JUSTICE.

Upon hearing the name Project Rescue, one might assume the ministry is engaged in social justice ("touching") but not in the biblical work of evangelism and discipleship. The same could be said of any number of compassion initiatives, i.e., Teen Challenge.[9] However, you can only ascertain a ministry's scope by looking at it closely, as we did in the chart for our own self-assessment. As accountable leaders of Project Rescue, we have established an ongoing intentionality to ensure the ministry is and remains consistent with the whole model of Jesus' teaching, preaching, and compassionate ministry. Jesus as Savior, and His message of redemption, remain at the heart of all aspects of Project Rescue's ministry. We believe intentionality and commitment to that approach to mission are the keys to life-changing compassion and justice.

4. THE LARGER AND MORE DEVELOPED A MINISTRY BECOMES—WHETHER A UNIVERSITY MINISTRY, LOCAL CHURCH, OR NONPROFIT MINISTRY—THE EASIER IT IS FOR THE EVANGELISM AND DISCIPLESHIP STREAMS OF THE MINISTRY TO BECOME SEPARATE FROM THE COMPASSIONATE STREAM.

The tendency is toward increasing specialization of ministries and away from holistic collaboration. In the process, if we aren't diligent, the proclaiming dimension of Jesus' Luke 4:18 mandate— "preaching the good news"—becomes more and more detached from the dimension of proclaiming freedom, healing, and releasing the oppressed. Instead of integration over time and organizational growth, we develop separate ministries that do specialized parts of what Jesus originally did as an integrated whole.

---

9   See http://teenchallengeusa.com/. Established by David Wilkerson in New York City in 1958, Teen Challenge is a nationally recognized, integrated, Christ-centered program of healing for those who struggle with substance abuse and addictions.

5. THE UNIQUE BEAUTY OF THE GOSPEL IS THAT THROUGH CHRIST, IT ADDRESSES THE NEEDS OF THE WHOLE PERSON: BODY, MIND, AND SPIRIT.

Proclamation and compassionate outreach were a seamless whole in Christ's life as He lovingly engaged the whole needs of people—sometimes starting with the physical or emotional dimension and other times with the spiritual dimension—but always life-changing, redeeming, and integrating. First and last and everywhere in between, Jesus must be at the heart of all we do in social justice and compassion ministries. Good people and agencies are rescuing slaves out of brothels, but only Jesus can take the impact of the brothel out of the slave's heart, mind, and spirit.

An artificial separation of compassion ministry from preaching and teaching God's truth undermines the integrity and potential transformational power of both. The integration of compassion ministries with Spirit-empowered preaching and discipleship packs a powerful punch! It reveals the face of an unconditionally loving heavenly Father—a disarming and nuanced glimpse of Him that those outside the body of Christ don't often see.

> First and last and everywhere in between, Jesus must be at the heart of all we do in social justice and compassion ministries.

Pastor Connie Weisel, women's pastor at First Assembly of God, Fort Myers, Florida, is one courageous lady who lives out the fullness of Christ's whole mission in her community. Committing her life fully to Christ at age thirty-eight, Connie was a successful businesswoman. Then, in 1991, she birthed a Monday night class out of First Assembly of God called "Help for Hurting Women" (HHW) to reach out to women like herself who needed a healing journey with Jesus. Women of all ages, social strata, and ethnic backgrounds came from all over southwest Florida for a night of praise, prayer, Bible study, and personal ministry. HHW has now met every single Monday night, except for national holidays, for twenty-three years! Over those years, 46,000 women have attended, with 3,450 coming to Christ for the first time or rededicating their lives to Him.

Pastor Connie concludes, "It's amazing how thousands have come to redemption and wholeness in such a simple setting. We have been faithful to 'just be there' week after week with love and comfort for women—no matter what their issues may be." But Pastor Connie and her leadership team don't wait for hurting women to find them. They are looking and led by the Spirit all week long, wherever their lives take them—to restaurants, grocery stores, workplaces—and invite women to meet them at HHW. Pastor Connie's team is sensitive for those who need Jesus and His help every day, wherever they find them. And women respond—coming from domestic violence, prostitution, broken marriages, and every kind of bondage imaginable. For thousands of women in Southwest Florida, HHW has been the beginning of their journey to salvation, healing, and a new life through Jesus.

CONCLUSION

The troubling question asked of K. K. Devaraj by the madam in Mumbai's Kamatapura red-light district several years ago is ultimately one that all of us must answer if God has called us to minister His love to people who are desperately broken: "Do you want her?"

Did K. K. want to be bothered with this woman who had been prostituted for years and experienced rape, violence, sexual abuse, and long-term trauma until she was mentally, physically, and spiritually destroyed?

Do we want her? If we see our Father's business exclusively in terms of evangelism and discipleship, probably not. This woman is far too complicated, her needs too great, her life too messy, the cost too high. At this point, she would probably not be able to come to our church services . . . and how would we get her there from where she is now? If we could pray with her, perhaps God would do a miracle and she could be instantaneously healed. Amazingly, God does those things sometimes, but many times He doesn't heal immediately. And if He didn't, how would we help this woman from the street?

What if we asked ourselves first if God wants her? What if we began to believe that the fragmented, naked woman on the street could one day become the glowing woman of grace in the purple sari, accepting a diploma for discipleship through tears of thanksgiving to God? What if we, as followers of Jesus, began to believe that women and men and boys and girls in horrific bondage really are our Father's business—and therefore ours as well?

Yes, what if we stopped splintering our Father's magnificent mission and caught a glimpse of His bold, life-changing compassion?

QUESTIONS FOR
COMPASSIONATE ENGAGEMENT

1. What has been your perspective on compassion ministry? How do you define compassion ministry?

2. Is your perspective one that integrates the proclaiming/preaching and compassionate dimensions of the church's missional mandate into a whole, or does it separate them into two categories: spiritual and physical? Which is more biblical and why?

3. If you were beginning a compassion ministry in your local community, what steps could you take to make sure it was authentically like Christ?

SUGGESTED LEARNING EXPERIENCE

With colleagues in a local ministry, local church, or small group, select a compassion ministry you participate in or are familiar with. Explore the following:

- What is its mission? Is it clearly articulated? Do team members know the mission?

- Is the mission connected to a local community of faith? In what way(s)?

- Together, diagram the focus of the compassion ministry and how it correlates with the components of the Great Commission to evangelize and disciple.

Is the ministry integrated with these or separate and/or parallel to them?

- If the ministry is integrated, explore how that can be strengthened to model Christ's example of integrated ministry more intentionally. If it is not integrated with ongoing evangelism and discipleship, consider why and how to integrate these elements, with practical steps that could be prayerfully accomplished.

FOR FURTHER STUDY

- Butrin, JoAnn. *From the Roots Up: A Closer Look at Compassion and Justice in Missions.* Springfield, MO: Roots Up Publishers, 2010.

- Lupton, Robert D. *Compassion, Justice and the Christian Life: Rethinking Ministry to the Poor.* Ventura, CA: Regal Books, 2007.

- Robb, Ruth, and Marion Carson (2002). *Working the Streets: A Handbook for Christians Involved in Outreach to Prostitutes.* Chichester, United Kingdom: New Wine Press, 2002.

- "The Bad Question of Proclamation vs. Social Action: A Symposium." *Evangelical Missions Quarterly* 48 no. 3 (July 2012): 264–271.

- "Pastor on a Mission Serving Poorest of the Poor." *Deccan Chronicle*, Bengaluru, India. Dec. 29, 2013, http://epaper.deccanchronicle.com/articledetailpage. aspx?id=249475.

CHAPTER 3

TWENTY-FIRST-CENTURY SEXUAL SLAVERY AND A BIBLICAL FOUNDATION FOR RESPONSE

But whenever anyone turns to the Lord, the veil is taken away. Now the Lord is the Spirit, and where the Spirit of the Lord is, there is freedom. And we all, who with unveiled faces contemplate the Lord's glory, are being transformed into his image with ever-increasing glory, which comes from the Lord, who is the Spirit.

2 CORINTHIANS 3:16–18

When outreach workers first began to visit the women and children in the city's brothels, Asha[10] was one of the first little girls they got to know. Although she was petite and appeared to be about six years old, her eyes were haunting and seemed much too old for her little-girl frame. Asha was her mother's caregiver. Whenever her mother was sick or needed an abortion, her young

---

10 Name has been changed for the sake of her security and dignity.

daughter was the one who accompanied her mother to the clinic, cooked the food, and nursed her lovingly back to health.

As ministry staff got to know Asha and her mother, they offered Asha a place in the aftercare home, along with several other little daughters from the red-light district. At first, this seemed totally impossible to both Asha and her mother. When this prostituted woman with serious medical issues needed care, who else in the world would take care of her? Both knew the answer: no one.

After many visits, much prayer, and growing trust, the day finally came when Asha's mother agreed to let her daughter go for the sake of an education and to escape from her inevitable fate in "the business." It took great courage in the face of threats of violence from her pimping husband for the mother to allow Asha to go into a new home and family of faith. This woman, who had absolutely no hope for herself, stood silently in the road and watched the car take her small daughter away to a new life in a Home of Hope. When the mother could see the car no more, she slowly turned and walked back alone into her world of slavery.

> The journey from slavery to freedom is never easy.

Within weeks, Asha responded to the love of Jesus for her and His promises for a different future. Along with several other little girls from the same red-light district, she began to receive the love and care of her newly-adopted spiritual mother, Vinita. Within weeks, she knew how to pray, worship God, and was motivated by faith to ask God to help her mom and meet her other needs. In fact, Asha became a natural leader among the little girls, and was quick to encourage other daughters still in the brothel to come to this wonderful new home. Staff began to see some moments of joy in the little girl's eyes—eyes that had been old, sad, and guarded. At first, these moments were few and far between. But over the next four years of healing, they have become more common for Asha as she finds peace in her new home, her new family, and her newly realized identity as a daughter of a loving heavenly Father.

But the journey from slavery to freedom is never easy. When Asha would return to visit her mom for special holidays, the home staff would pray for her protection, knowing her mom would be threatened physically to keep her daughter from returning to the aftercare home. The healthier and more educated this growing girl became, the more buyers of sex would be willing to pay her mother's pimp for sex with her. Once, when Asha did not return after the holiday, the staff knew she was in danger of being lost back to this evil system. Prayerfully, they went again and again to pick her up, but without success. They were amazed one day when they received a hurried, desperate call from the little girl. Her mother had fallen asleep under the influence of alcohol, and Asha had found her cell phone and called the staff to come get her quickly. She wanted to come "home"! The staff and the other children celebrated this feisty little fighter's return to safety.

This year, Asha has become a young woman of fourteen, and the journey of hope and healing continues in her new family. It has not been easy. The staff received news that Asha's mom, who had grown more and more sickly, was at last found dead on a road near her village. No one claimed to know what happened to her. Asha, her daughter—her caregiver—

> There are some hurts in wounded hearts that only time and God can heal.

has had to deal with knowing she was not there to help. There are some hurts in wounded hearts that only time and God can heal.

But the God who loves orphans loves Asha. He still has power to heal the brokenhearted and bind up their wounds (Ps. 147:3). Asha continues to mature, and exhibits natural leadership gifts and courage. Her adopted spiritual moms and big sisters see the potential of a "Deborah"[11] in the making. Asha may well become a voice to speak hope and salvation on behalf of those still enslaved in bondage and exploitation. She knows slavery personally; she has found freedom in Jesus; and Asha has the courage to fight!

GLOBAL SEX TRAFFICKING:
THE NEW SLAVERY

Trafficking in persons for the purposes of sexual exploitation, especially in women and children, is quickly becoming the world's fastest growing industry and most profitable criminal activity. As far back as the *2002 Human Rights Report on Trafficking in Persons*,[12] it was documented that virtually every nation in the world is engaged to some extent in this tragic trade, whether as a country of origin, transit, or destination for victims. UNICEF estimates that one million children alone are forced, sold, abducted, or coerced into the commercial sex trade annually. Solid figures are difficult to come by. Estimates of women and children trafficked across international borders each year range anywhere from 800,000 to 4,000,000.[13]

---

11 The story of Deborah, the prophetess, is found in Judges 4. It recounts Deborah's obedience in victoriously leading the army of God's people into battle against their enemy, King Jabin.

12 *The Protection Project, 2002 Human Rights Report on Trafficking in Persons*. Paul H. Nitze School of Advanced International Studies, Johns Hopkins University, 2002.

13 Jennifer Goodson, "Exploiting Body and Soul," *Sojourners Magazine*, September/ October 2005.

And in the United States, the US State Department estimates that as many as 18,500 men, women, and children are trafficked into the nation each year, many for sexual exploitation (2004). Out of trafficked persons globally, the US Department of State reports that 80 percent are believed to be women and children.[14]

> Unfortunately, current political, economic, and social factors in our world create a fertile environment for ruthless traffickers who prey on vulnerable victims.

As for profitability, human trafficking has exploded into a $12 billion-per-year global industry,[15] with sex trafficking constituting a major part. A girl who is purchased by a trafficker for as little as $150 can be sold to customers as many as ten times a night, bringing in $10,000 a month profit.[16] With minimal overhead expense, police as co-predators, and almost unlimited numbers of victims on whom to prey, trafficking for sexual exploitation is surpassing the sale of illegal drugs as the preferred industry for criminals.

Sex trafficking is officially defined as the movement of women and children, within national or across international borders, for the purposes of prostitution or other forms of commercial sexual exploitation. It includes the recruitment, transportation, harboring, transfer, or sale of women and children for these purposes. The

---

14 Mary C. Burke, *Human Trafficking: Interdisciplinary Perspectives* (New York: Routledge, 2013), xxviii.

15 Gilbert King, *Woman, Child for Sale: The New Slave Trade in the Twenty-First Century* (New York: Penguin Group, 2004), 19.

16 Kevin Bales, *Disposable People: New Slavery in the Global Economy* (Los Angeles, CA: University of California Press,1999).

ultimate end of sexual trafficking is brutality, sexual slavery, and not infrequently, death.

Unfortunately, current political, economic, and social factors in our world create a fertile environment for ruthless traffickers who prey on vulnerable victims. To illustrate, in 2005, one-third of all sex trafficking occurring in the world was taking place in nations that were formerly part of the Soviet Union.[17] Out of the economic and moral chaos that followed the USSR's collapse, staggering numbers of young women and girls living in poverty were easily lured by false promises of lucrative jobs in Western Europe. Others are abducted outright in areas of Moldova, Romania, and Bulgaria as they walk from school along country roads.[18] In Moldova in particular, a despicable pattern of trafficking targets the thousands of girls who live in state orphanages when they are released as teenagers. Malarek documents that traffickers know the exact timing of the sixteen- and seventeen-year-old orphans' release, and are there to meet them when they leave and have nowhere else to go. In all of the trafficking schemes, once the new victims' legal papers are submitted into their new "bosses'" possession, the victims quickly lose their freedom and any illusions of a better life. Enslavement follows in brothels of international cities across Western Europe, where new "sex workers" are raped and brutalized until they are willing to submit to their new roles as sex slaves.

As Kevin Bales' research documents, extreme poverty is where slavery grows best.[19] But other cultural, social, and religious factors

---

17 Dr. Kent Hill, USAID Assistant Administrator for Europe and Eurasia, in presentation to Consortium of Faith-Based Initiatives on Human Trafficking, Washington, DC, 2005.

18 Victor Malarek, *The Natashas: Inside the New Global Sex Trade.* (New York: Arcade Publishing, 2003).

19 Bales, 31.

also contribute to the proliferation of the tragedy of sex trafficking and pursuant slavery.

- Wars and natural disasters around the world turn women and children into refugees who are especially vulnerable to victimization as they flee for their lives.

- Globalization has facilitated the transport of goods and services across international borders, including the transport of human cargo and sexual services.

- Times of political upheaval are accompanied by the upheaval of traditional family and community support systems. Presumed protectors become predators, and the human rights of the weakest and most vulnerable are savagely trampled with little to no recourse.

- Within traditional Islamic and Hindu cultures, women and daughters are viewed as property, financial liabilities, social burdens, and even children of a lesser god. As a result, daughters and wives may be neglected, underfed, undereducated, abused, and sold as property. Their primary significance as persons is derived from their relationships with the male members of their families, whether fathers, husbands, or sons. A woman's value is associated with her ability to bear a child, particularly a male child. Her life and future are to a great extent in the hands of men.

- The burgeoning global appetites for child sex, homosexuality, pornography, and sex tourism are creating an insatiable demand for sex slaves.

- With the global AIDS crisis, affluent customers looking for sexual services with virgins are driving the market for younger and younger victims.

- Commercial sexual exploitation has become more decentralized, with an explosion of global technology making it increasingly difficult for law enforcement, government agencies, and would-be helpers to address. Burke points out that while sex trafficking in the past was more localized in brothels and identifiable red-light districts, sexual exploitation now occurs in many settings, including hotels and nightclubs.[20]

As if the injustice of trafficking and sexual slavery were not sufficiently deplorable, the tragedy only multiplies as its targets are routinely victimized again and again in the political and "justice" systems of the world. Often when trafficked women are taken in police raids at brothels, they are treated as criminals or illegal immigrants and either charged and imprisoned or deported—literally dumped—back to their own countries. Ironically, the traffickers and pimps remain free to prey on newer and younger victims.

The good news is that in the past ten years, good people around the world who respect the dignity of human life have become aware of this horrible global injustice. And in the process

---

20 Burke, 61.

of focusing on the epic battle that must be waged, a fascinating fact has come to light. Evangelical Christian organizations around the world have been on the cutting edge of awareness of the horrible injustice and have proven quick to respond.[21] Frequently working under the political and media "radar" to avoid publicity and to protect victims from being revictimized, a number of international Christian ministries like the International Salvation Army, World Hope (the compassionate arm of the Wesleyan Methodist Church), World Relief (National Association of Evangelicals), Assemblies of God World Missions, and Catholic Relief Services, among others, have been working quietly to bring freedom and restoration to women and children in sexual slavery. In the May 21, 2002 edition of the *New York Times*, writer Nicholas Kristof noted this trend and called evangelicals "America's new internationalists,"[22] especially in spearheading political and legislative action to fight this battle against sex trafficking. Why have people of faith been drawn to engage in this battle and why are they so ready to minister to its victims?

A BIBLICAL FOUNDATION FOR MINISTRY TO VICTIMS OF SEXUAL SLAVERY

The Jewish social activist Michael Horowitz documents that evangelical Christians have historically been the ones who risked everything to go to the difficult places in our world and care for the most vulnerable victims of injustice and poverty. The evangelical Christian response to the tragedy of sex trafficking and slavery has

---

21 Michael Horowitz, "How to Win Friends and Influence Culture," *Christianity Today,* September 2005, 71–78.

22 Nicholas Kristof, "Following God Abroad," *The New York Times,* May 21, 2002.

> Each man, woman, and child is equally deserving of love, respect, and dignity.

been no exception. Horowitz rightly contends that engaging in this issue is inherent to the Christian identity and belief system. Let's look at some of the most basic biblical themes that compel people of faith to address twenty-first-century sexual slavery and bring Christ's love to victims of all forms of sexual exploitation. God's perspective on the value of women and the girl child is given special attention because of its significance to a Christian perspective as compared to other belief systems, and because the majority of sexually exploited persons are women and girls.

THE BIBLE TEACHES THE DIGNITY OF ALL HUMAN LIFE [23]

We believe that all life is created by God and stamped with His image (Gen. 1:27). That image has been marred by sin but can be restored by the redemptive work of Jesus Christ and God's love (2 Cor. 5:17; Gal. 3:26). Each individual is unique in God's creation, endowed with God-given gifts and God-ordained purpose. As such, each man, woman, and child is equally deserving of love, respect, and dignity (Gal. 3:28–29).

---

23 Adapted from Beth Grant, Catherine Clark Kroeger, and Joni Middleton, "Unit 3: A Biblical Framework for a Christian Response to Human Trafficking," in *Hands that Heal: International Curriculum to Train Caregivers of Trafficking Survivors, Academic Version* (Baltimore, MD: FAAST, 2007).

GOD IS A GOD OF JUSTICE, AND HE BLESSES THOSE WHO MAINTAIN JUSTICE

The theme of justice runs strongly throughout the Old Testament. The Lord is righteous and loves justice (Deut. 32:4; Ps. 11:7; Isa. 61:8). All God's ways are just (Deut. 32:4; 2 Chron. 19:7), and He blesses those who maintain justice (Ps. 106:3; Isa. 56:1; Zech. 7:9). Conversely, God has strong warnings for those who perpetrate injustice (Prov. 28; Luke 11:42).

GOD CREATED WOMAN AND THE GIRL CHILD AND GAVE THEM INHERENT DIGNITY AND VALUE

Why do girls matter? Why are the lives of women and children worth fighting for? According to the creation account in Genesis, woman is a creation of God (Gen. 1:27; Mark 10:6; 1 Cor. 11:13), lovingly made in His very own image and likeness (Gen. 1:26; 5:1). She was created as an equal partner and helper for man, to serve God with him (Gen. 2:18). God blessed the woman He created (Gen. 5:2) and gave her authority with man over the other life forms He had fashioned (Gen. 1:28–30). God saw woman as a part of His creation, and He valued her as good in His eyes (Gen.1:31).

The value God places on His female creation is revealed in the roles He ordained them to fill in accomplishing His eternal purposes at pivotal moments in the history of His people. Miriam, the sister of Moses and Aaron, was called by God as a prophetess and leader during the Israelites' exodus from Egypt (Exod. 15:21). Deborah, a prophetess and wife of Lappidoth, was chosen by God to lead the Israelites into victorious battle against the Canaanites (Judges 4). Ruth, a Moabite woman, established herself in Israel's history by becoming the ancestress of King David (Ruth 4:18–22) and Jesus Christ (Matt. 1:1, 5). The Jewess Esther was sovereignly ordained by God to become queen in a land of exile in order to deliver His people from destruction (Esther 4:14).

The record of the New Testament is just as illuminating in the ways God used women as instruments of His purposes in the life and ministry of Jesus. God's favor on the young Mary was dramatically pronounced by an angel, who announced that she would give birth to the incarnate Son of God (Luke 1:30, 31). After His birth, the elderly prophetess Anna attended the infant Jesus' presentation at the temple and announced the significance of His birth "to all those who were looking forward to the redemption of Jerusalem" (Luke 2:36–38).

> Jesus demonstrated respect and concern for women in a culture that relegated them to secondary, even menial, status.

During the terrifying hours of Jesus' crucifixion, as the earth shook in agony, Mary Magdalene, Mary the mother of James and Joseph, and the mother of the sons of Zebedee faithfully stayed to attend their dying Lord (Matt. 27:55–56). After Jesus' death, it was devoted women disciples who followed to the place where His body was taken, returned with spices for burial, and discovered that He had risen from the dead (Luke 23:55–56; 24:1–6). Theirs was the joy of first announcing the message of Jesus' resurrection that would forever change the course of human destiny!

If how one treats others corresponds to the value one places on them, the manner in which Jesus treated women during His life on earth was significant. As He traveled with His disciples through

Samaria, Jesus demonstrated His value for a Samaritan woman at the well by engaging her in conversation and revealing His identity as the Messiah (John 4:26). In spite of His disciples' surprise at His behavior, and the woman's less-than-circumspect reputation, Jesus' actions spoke clearly that the Samaritan woman was worthy of hearing and receiving God's truth and sharing it with others in her community. Amazingly to those who watched, this woman mattered to the Son of God.

Jesus demonstrated respect and concern for women in a culture that relegated them to secondary, even menial, status. For example, His relationship with Mary and Martha is demonstrated in His concern for them at their brother's death (John 11). The way the sisters freely related their frustrations and fears to Jesus speaks to the level of friendship that He shared with them, as well as with their brother (John 11:21, 28, 32.)

Another meaningful glimpse of Jesus' awareness of and concern for women is provided in Luke 13:10–17. While teaching in a synagogue, the Master Teacher caught sight of a woman who had been crippled for eighteen years. Calling her to Himself, He laid His hands on her and healed her—to the indignation of those watching. Rebuking His critics for their hypocrisy, Jesus honored the rejoicing woman with a reminder that she was "a daughter of Abraham," deserving of the freedom from bondage that He bestowed.

In Luke 8, both a young girl who had died and an older woman with a twelve-year history of bleeding are the focus of the compassionate Son of God. While on His way to pray over Jairus' young daughter, Jesus sensed that healing had come to someone in the crowd who had touched Him. Knowing, in fact, who had touched Him, the Lord nonetheless called the woman with the issue of blood out of the crowd and commended her publicly for her great faith (Luke 8:47–48).

Even a woman who was to be stoned for adultery by the religious leaders of the day was treated with concern and dignity by the Son of God. The apostle John records a dramatic scene in which the woman was physically forced before Jesus by the accusing Pharisees (John 8:1–11). When questioned about what this sinful woman's fate should be, Jesus did not add to her humiliation. Instead, He addressed her directly, recognizing her sin without condemning her, and offered her a future free from the bondage of sin. Yes, by His consistently compassionate actions toward them and a willingness to include them in His life and ministry, Jesus consistently revealed that women were created as daughters of God and were intended recipients of His love and redemptive work.

After Jesus' death and resurrection, it was left to His disciples to carry on His work empowered by the promised Holy Spirit (Acts 1:14; 2:4). According to the record of New Testament writers, women were called along with men, and were gifted and empowered by God for diverse ministries within the early church. Among the women named and commended for their active role were: Priscilla, a teacher and coworker with the apostle Paul (Rom. 16:3; Acts 18:23–28); Phoebe, a deaconess (Rom 16:1–2); and Junia, an apostle (Rom. 16:7). Throughout Paul's writings, a number of women are commended for their help in the ministries of the fledgling church (Rom. 16:1–12). It is evident that women were not only created by God and recipients of Christ's redemption, but were also an integral part of the Spirit-empowered ministries of the first-century body of Christ.

THE REDEMPTIVE POWER OF JESUS CHRIST WAS INTENDED FOR BODY, MIND, AND SPIRIT

By both His recorded words and actions, Jesus demonstrated that He came to earth to bring healing and new life not only to the spirit but to the whole person as uniquely created by God: body, soul, and spirit. As He proclaimed Himself the Bread of Life through whom all who believe can live throughout eternity (John 6:48–51), the Son of God tangibly demonstrated His concern for the physical, emotional, mental, and relational well-being of His creation. The following illustrations from Scripture reveal the transforming ministry of Jesus Christ to all dimensions of people's lives.

PHYSICAL HEALING

As Jesus left Jericho, he encountered two blind men by the side of the road. He responded to their cries for help and miraculously gave them sight (Matt. 20:29–34). The Gospels are rich with stories in which the physical plight of men, women, and children were met with Jesus' compassionate healing response.

SPIRITUAL HEALING

An anguished father brought his son, who had been controlled all of his life by evil spirits, to Jesus. The demonic power that tormented the boy with violent seizures was cast out by Jesus' loving power, and his health was restored (Mark 9:17–27).

EMOTIONAL HEALING

The woman at the well in Samaria whom Jesus engaged in conversation was living in a series of sexual relationships, implying relational failure, spiritual death, and social alienation. Rather than perpetuating her social alienation and devaluing her because of her failures, Jesus spoke into her life with the truth of who He was as the Messiah. The woman, who would normally have avoided social interaction in her community, ran back excitedly to announce her life-changing encounter with the Son of God (John 4:1–26).

RELATIONAL HEALING

Perhaps one of the greatest images of relational healing of all time is that of the prodigal son described by Jesus in Luke 15. It is the ultimate story of a loving Father who grieves over a lost son who has left home on a journey of self-destruction. When the son comes to his senses and realizes he is wasting his life and his father's resources, he turns his steps home in repentance. Expecting less than a son's welcome, his father sees him and runs to welcome him home with full forgiveness and restoration of relationship. The forgiving, restoring, loving father is a powerful image for broken humanity everywhere who has lost relationship with their heavenly Father. In Matthew 22:37, Jesus declared that the greatest commandment of all is to "Love the Lord your God with all your heart and with all your soul and with all your mind." This ultimate purpose for all men, women, and children can only be attained when they have been touched in every dimension of their lives by the loving power of the Son of God.

THE GREAT COMMISSION MANDATE AND ACCOMPANYING EMPOWERMENT

In Matthew 28:18–20, Jesus gave His last recorded instructions to His disciples before He departed for heaven. Evangelical Christians have embraced His words as the priority mandate for the church down through history:

> All authority in heaven and on earth has been given to me. Therefore go and make disciples of all nations, baptizing them in the name of the Father and of the Son and of the Holy Spirit, and teaching them to obey everything I have commanded you.

"All nations" includes men, women, and children of every people group, language, caste, and class, regardless of economic, social, and religious categories. For twenty-first-century Christians who become aware of the plight of millions of exploited women and children caught in the horrendous evil of sexual slavery, the Great Commission of Jesus compels us to go, preach, and act to bring new life to victims through Jesus Christ—wherever they are, whatever their condition. Evangelical believers take seriously the life-changing promise in 2 Corinthians 5:17 that if any man or woman be "in Christ" they are a new creation. It applies not only to the educated woman in a corporate boardroom; it applies as well to the prostituted teenager dying of AIDS who believes in Christ.

But how does one confront this darkest and most dangerous face of evil called sexual slavery and see victims' lives supernaturally changed? For Pentecostal Christians around the world, empowerment and direction for life-changing obedience to Jesus' mandate are found through the work of the Holy Spirit. In Acts 1:8, Jesus promised that when His disciples received the promised Holy Spirit in the upper room, they would receive power to carry on His message and transforming work both locally and globally. The miracles of the book of Acts are a testimony to the fulfillment of that promise.

> The power of God to work through followers of Jesus continues today in the rescue and restoration of victims of sexual slavery.

The power of God to work through followers of Jesus continues today in the rescue and restoration of victims of sexual slavery. The words of Jesus announcing His earthly ministry have become the burning testimony of His followers who minister to brutalized women and children around the world:

> The Spirit of the Lord is upon me, because He has anointed me to preach good news to the poor. He has sent me to proclaim freedom for the prisoners and recovery of sight for the blind, to release the oppressed, to proclaim the year of the Lord's favor.
> (Luke 4:18–19)

CONCLUSION

Bryant Myers, respected missiologist working with global development, describes the goals of transformation in working with the poor and vulnerable as well as the nonpoor. He contends this transformational journey is "to recover our true identity as human beings created in the image of God and to discover our true vocation as productive stewards, faithfully caring for the world and all the people in it."[24] Myers' definition captures a strong theology of God as the giver of life, purpose, and vocation, and of every person's potential to become faithful stewards of God's life and resources. What a faith-filled prophetic vision of transformation for all who are considered less valuable in human eyes—especially those who have been victims of the injustice of sexual slavery.

24 Bryant Myers, *Walking with the Poor: Principles and Practices of Transformational Development* (Maryknoll, NY: Orbis Books, 1999), 3.

SUGGESTED LEARNING EXPERIENCE

Within your small group or class, discuss the following:

- Revisit the facts about the injustice of sexual slavery
  in the chapter. Discuss additional information that
  members of your group can share related to this
  injustice in your nation and city. What particular
  factors are encouraging sexual exploitation in
  your culture?

- Are you surprised to learn that followers of Jesus
  globally have been on the front edge of responding
  to sex trafficking and the needs of victims? Discuss
  why or why not.

- There are strong condemning words in the Old
  Testament regarding prostitutes and women
  who have been sexually violated. Look at specific
  references beginning with the tragic story of Tamar
  in 2 Samuel 13: 1–22. How does this perspective
  compare with: a) the view of your culture, and b) the
  life and teaching of Jesus? Give Scriptural references.

- Review the way God views women and sees their
  value according to Scripture. While it is easy to
  see how the value of women is distorted in other
  cultures, consider how the value of women has
  become distorted in your own culture. How is it in
  conflict with the value God places on His daughters,
  as demonstrated by Jesus?

- Develop together some action steps as a group for valuing girls and women in your personal life, family, and church community as daughters of God created by Him with inherent gifts for His good purposes.

FOR FURTHER STUDY

- Burke, Mary C. *Human Trafficking: Interdisciplinary Perspectives*. New York: Routledge, 2013.
- Kilbourn, Phyllis. *Shaping the Future: Girls and Our Destiny*. Pasadena, CA: William Carey Library, 2008.

CHAPTER 4

PROJECT RESCUE'S JOURNEY: MISSION, MIRACLES, AND MISTAKES

There is no value-free social response to human need and injustice. All human response to human need and injustice is inevitably influenced by the values and worldview of the person responding—whether Muslim, Hindu, Buddhist, atheist, liberal Democrat, or conservative Republican.

Then it should be no surprise, but assumed, that any initiative focused on the injustice of sexual slavery and the restoration of victims developed by a Christian organization or mission should reflect the person and message of Jesus Christ. Let's do compassion and justice with excellence and integrity—but let's not be apologetic about who we are and the One whose perfect love compels us to act.[25]

Out of the first encounter in 1997 of Bombay Teen Challenge (BTC) outreach workers and Assemblies of God World

---

25 Shared by author at an anti-trafficking consortium meeting of government and nongovernment participants in Washington, DC, 2006.

Missions with the brutal world of sexual slavery in Mumbai, the ministry of Project Rescue was born. The thirty-seven little girls given to Director K. K. Devaraj and his staff by their prostituted mothers became the urgent impetus for committed partnership between BTC and Assemblies of God World Missions (AGWM) personnel to address the needs of those in sexual slavery in India. At the time, the term *sex trafficking* was not in the vocabulary of anyone we knew. Only years later did we learn that *trafficked* was the official legal term for almost every woman and child we met in India's red-light districts. Our burning purpose was to minister Christ's love, healing, and transforming truth to broken women and children in slavery, rather than to address the trafficking issue *per se*. When looking into the faces of desperate women or children devastated by the violence in the brothels, our primary concern was not how they got there. It was how to help them get out of there and receive a new life through the One who loves them most. That priority has never changed.

The first of many faith steps in the journey was the aftercare home for the thirty-seven daughters of prostituted women on Falkland Road. It was a leased, temporary place of safety, healing, and loving care. That was the unexpected beginning of what would become a multi-faceted network of affiliated Christian ministries to victims of sexual slavery and their children in India, Nepal, Bangladesh, Tajikistan, Moldova, and Spain. In 2013, those affiliated ministries miraculously touched the lives of over 32,000 women and children in Jesus' name.

PROJECT RESCUE'S THREE-PRONG STRATEGY: INTERVENTION, RESTORATION, AND PREVENTION

INTERVENTION

Intervention includes efforts to rescue women and children from the slavery of prostitution. Intervention can take different forms:

- Negotiating the release of enslaved women and girls from brothels through relationships in the community.

- Accepting trafficking victims who've been rescued during police raids into safe homes for healing aftercare.

- Intervening to get the children of prostituted women out of the brothels and out of harm's way during their mothers' peak work hours and into night-care centers or after-school programs. Like a traditional Christian daycare center, these ministry sites include a safe bed, food, a loving community, tutoring for school work, prayer, discipleship, and Jesus. The children hear stories about God's love for them and His power to change their lives and fulfill the dreams He has placed in their hearts.

- Connecting with prostituted women and children through medical clinics or vocational training centers to provide important needed help, build relationships, and give opportunity to begin their spiritual journey. In one city in particular, the vocational unit has become a safe place where women still living in the brothels can begin to make a different living, enabling them to become financially viable and pay back their own "debts" in order to get out of trafficking. The VU, as it is known, has also become their functioning church since that is where they have met Jesus and are discipled to follow Him week by week.

During the first year, Project Rescue helped to pay off some of the women's "debts" to the brothel owners or their madams in order to attain their release. However, as ministry leaders began to understand how the exploitive systems of prostitution work, they realized that this strategy only put well-intentioned money back into the hands of organized crime and procurers to obtain other young sex slaves. In the following sixteen years of Project Rescue's ministries, the practice of paying off prostituted women's "debts" is done only as a last resort. Most often, the release of women and children has been negotiated over time in Southern Asia without the exchange of money, because the intervention initiatives are national-led, community-based, and relationship-maintained.

To illustrate, whenever possible, personal working relationships are established with police, city government officials, and even brothel owners (all for whom Jesus also died). Because of the outreach workers' willingness to minister to everyone in the red-light district, they become known for their genuine compassionate demonstration of Christ's love in tangible ways. As a result, when an enslaved woman asks for help to get out of "the business," staff can go to the madam or brothel owner and appeal to them based on their relationship with them—as the friend who has also prayed for them and their children. In this way, the very perception of a ministry exchanging money for women and children's lives is avoided, because the whole injustice of sexual slavery is based on that dehumanizing economic exchange.

As Project Rescue-affiliated ministries have grown and earned respect, police at times contact ministry directors when a raid has been conducted in the red-light district and girls have been taken into custody. Aftercare for victims rescued in police raids, in some countries, is minimal at best. It is not unusual for rescued girls and women to be held at police stations, raped and brutalized again, and sent back to the brothel owners to be put back to "work." Would-be protectors have become predators themselves. Given this reality, Project Rescue ministry leaders are thankful when police inform them of raids and give them the opportunity to intervene with aftercare in a safe place of healing and hope.

RESTORATION

Restoration addresses the physical, emotional, mental, and educational needs of rescued women and girls as they are discipled to a new life in Jesus Christ. Restoration includes the following components offered onsite or in collaboration with other service providers:

- General medical care
- Counseling for the trauma of abuse and exploitation
- Basic literacy training
- Prayer (including prayer for deliverance from demonic power), worship, learning God's Word, and Christian discipleship

- Vocational training leading to
  financial independence

- Hospice care for women dying of HIV/AIDS and
  related illnesses

In Southern Asia, women in sex slavery in the red-light districts have been willing to relinquish their daughters to outreach workers so they could escape the horrors of the brothels before the mothers themselves had the courage to try to escape. Women who have been prostituted for years in violence and intimidation don't believe there is any hope for themselves for a different life. Prostitution has become their identity. However, when mothers of daughters in the programs observe how ministry staff love and care for their children, and see their children flourishing, trust begins to grow between Project Rescue workers and mothers still in slavery. Over months and even years, many mothers have gained courage to request help and start their own journeys out of slavery toward physical, spiritual, and emotional freedom. Rescued daughters learn how to pray and cry out to God daily for their mothers' freedom and salvation. It's a day of celebration when those beloved mothers in prostitution take their first steps toward deliverance!

> The most effective and powerful workers in Bombay Teen Challenge ministry today are former madams who were rescued from the brothels ten to twelve years ago and restored into a new life in Christ.

An increasingly high percentage of the women being rescued through Project Rescue-affiliated ministries in India are HIV-positive, or already suffer from AIDS. Generally, because they have been in prostitution, they are not welcomed back by their families or communities. In such cases, aftercare home staff and other rescued women in the restoration process become their new family of faith. They are the ones who surround their sisters in Christ with love, dignity, and support as they leave this life that has been so tragic and go into God's presence. Sad, yes; but thankfully they go into God's presence with *dignity, hope,* and *respect* and into the eternal home He has prepared for those who love Him. Without the compassionate ministries of Jesus' followers, they *would* die in shame, hopelessness, and indignity in the streets, discarded by the destructive system they can no longer profit. One day, we will see these daughters of God at the marriage supper of the Lamb. Thank God, there will be no more sin, trauma, stigma, or violence there!

The most effective and powerful workers in Bombay Teen Challenge ministry today are former madams who were rescued from the brothels ten to twelve years ago and restored into a new life in Christ. They fearlessly go back into their former places of slavery and work to bring other enslaved women out of bondage. One diminutive former madam, who is particularly respected in the district and has a powerful ministry, was formerly known for having formidable evil power. During annual Hindu festivals, she was carried in the ritual processions to represent the goddesses. Now this transformed woman is using her God-given leadership and management skills and God's creative power to bring other women out of sexual slavery and help them grow into strong women of God. He is doing miracles!

PREVENTION

Prevention takes several forms in the Project Rescue strategy:

- Providing safe houses for sex slaves' young daughters before they, too, are forced into sexual slavery at eleven and twelve years of age.

- Conducting AIDS awareness and sex trafficking awareness projects in the high-risk areas of Western Nepal and North India.

- Intervening in the sale of daughters to traffickers.

Aftercare homes established for the young daughters of prostituted women directly save these daughters from a life of prostitution in the brothels. Daughters are placed in ministry aftercare homes at the mother's request, with her permission, or by a madam or relative in the district when the child's mother dies. Ongoing contact between the mother and child is encouraged by the staff, and the whole "family" of staff and children pray regularly for the mothers who are still enslaved. Little daughters whom society and families believe are destined for sexual exploitation are loved, cared for in a safe place, and educated to become the strong women of God He created them to be.

Over the years, a second strategic aspect of prevention for Project Rescue has developed in the western areas of Nepal. Procurers who traffic Nepali girls into Indian brothels go to the same poverty-stricken areas to convince families to sell their daughters. Project Rescue, in partnership with the Nepali Assemblies of God churches and other NGOs, has conducted community awareness projects to educate families in high-risk areas of the tragedies of girl-trafficking and AIDS. Initiatives have included establishing bases for adult awareness, basic literacy training for girl children, medical clinics, and spiritual outreach into the local community.

As the affiliated ministries of Project Rescue became known and respected in North India and other ministry sites, another opportunity for prevention presented itself. Project Rescue workers have been confidentially notified by concerned villagers when a family is in the process of negotiating the sale of their daughter to traffickers. Through negotiations, ministry workers have been able to intervene and prevent the sale of a number of young girls into sexual slavery by offering financial help to the impoverished parents and arranging to place their daughter in a Christian home or reputable children's group home.

THE ESSENTIAL ROLE OF THE CHURCH

It is impossible to describe the strategy and any success of Project Rescue in Southern Asia, Nepal, or Spain in ministering to victims of sexual slavery and trafficking without including the crucial component of the local church. While the church doesn't fit neatly under any one of the three prongs in the ministry's strategy, in actuality, it is incorporated into all three.

Intervention in the lives of women in sexual slavery in Mumbai occurs every Saturday afternoon in an old Anglican church at the edge of the Falkland Road red-light district. There, as many as several hundred women and children come from the nearby brothels to hear "Uncle" Devaraj preach the good news of Jesus' love for them and His power to change their lives.

> Supernatural faith for men, women, and children still comes through the God-ordained process of hearing God's Word.

Restoration begins as a spiritual journey in the old church as prostituted women and madams respond for prayer week after week. Many, like the demoniacs whom Jesus delivered while on earth, need His healing touch for deliverance. They need prayer for faith to believe that there is Someone they can trust who will not—ever!—betray them. Women who have lived most of their young lives as sex slaves need tremendous courage to dare try to escape the intimidation of organized crime. They are racked with questions such as, "Where would I go?" and "How could the mafia not find me?" Among the caring Bombay Teen Challenge workers, rescued children, and former sex slaves who have found freedom and gather on Saturday nights for a church service, women still in slavery experience prayer, faith, and hope to take the first steps in the journey toward their own personal freedom. Yes, supernatural faith for men, women, and children still comes through the God-ordained process of hearing God's Word (Rom. 10:17), even for those enslaved in prostitution.

Prevention miraculously occurs for young victims and their daughters when they find the old Anglican church in their earliest days of sexual slavery. The sooner they find freedom in Jesus, the better their chance of a life and death without AIDS. Prevention also takes place as churches in high-risk areas all over Southern Asia become aware of the injustice of sex trafficking and help local families protect their daughters from becoming entrapped.

Local national churches partnering with Project Rescue-affiliated ministries fill another key role. Godly local women who speak the language, understand the local culture, can keep a low profile in the district, and have a heart for victimized women are ideal staff for the ministry. While missionaries can be key partners in casting vision, challenging destructive cultural practices, raising needed funds, and playing support roles in ministry initiatives, they are generally not as effective long-term in the day-to-day red-light district outreach. Pioneers for Project Rescue in India, Nepal, Bangladesh, Tajikistan, Moldova, and Spain have been compassionate national Christian women leaders in local churches who have a burden for exploited women and are willing to invest their time, skills, and resources to aid in their restoration over the long term.

It's thrilling to see Project Rescue-affiliated ministries now coming full circle. Young girls who were rescued out of the red-light districts ten to fifteen years ago have come successfully through the healing process. A number of them from Mumbai and Pune have graduated from school and feel called of God to minister to children still in the red-light districts. They are now becoming key staff members in ministries like the one that brought Jesus and freedom to them. This small but growing army of young women have been rescued and redeemed and are now participating with God's mission to see others find freedom as well. Every transformed girl is a miracle!

Practical political reality also requires local ministers and staff to be the foundation of ministries to prostituted women and children globally. Sexual slavery and trafficking are almost always controlled by brutal organized crime, often in cooperation with local police, local governments, or even national government officials in power. The visible presence of foreign workers in areas of prostitution can draw dangerous negative attention, not only to the foreign worker, but also to the local ministry, local staff ,and the women and children whom we are trying to help. The extent of political danger varies from country to country, and even from region to region within the same country. There are some notable exceptions of expatriate women being called of God to break ground in these kinds of ministries in their host cultures—women like pioneers Lauran Bethell[26] and Patricia Green.[27] However, our experience has been that they are the exception rather than the norm. The goal of these pioneers is generally to turn leadership of the initiative over to national directors as soon as possible for the sake of long-term ministry sustainability.

MISTAKES WE HAVE MADE

Mistakes are not fun to experience. However, sometimes they are good to share, for several reasons. First, recounting the times we "missed it"—especially as ministers and followers of Jesus—helps us remember not to take ourselves too seriously, and if and when things work out well, we know God deserves the credit.

Secondly, people tend to make heroes out of "earthen vessels," which is how Paul described believers like us:

---

26 Lauran Bethell is a missionary with American Baptist International Ministries who has been working for more than two decades on behalf of women who have been exploited and abused. As the first Director of the New Life Center in Chiang Mai in the north of Thailand (1987), Lauran pioneered projects in Southeast Asia that specifically addressed the issue of child prostitution and trafficking of women and children. The Center was started with eighteen residents in an effort to offer young tribal women an opportunity to receive an education and vocational training, which provided alternatives to prostitution and other forms of exploitation.

27 Patricia Green is a social worker and ordained minister with the Assemblies of God New Zealand, and has a master's degree in Community Psychology. She has served as founder/director of: Landmark Christian Homes for Girls, Hamilton, New Zealand (1971–1987), Rahab Ministries, Bangkok, Thailand (1988–2004), and Alabaster Jar, Berlin, Germany, an outreach to women in street prostitution (2006 to the present).

For we do not preach ourselves, but Christ Jesus the Lord, and ourselves your bondservants for Jesus' sake. For it is the God who commanded light to shine out of darkness, who has shone in our hearts to give the light of the knowledge of the glory of God in the face of Jesus Christ. But we have this treasure in earthen vessels, that the excellence of the power may be of God and not of us (2 Cor. 4:5–7, NKJV).

"Earthen vessels" is Paul's (and God's) metaphoric way of saying we are very human and prone to inglorious lives and all-too-human actions. What sets followers of Jesus apart? The "treasure" of God's glory that has come to reside in us through the life-changing power of Jesus. What does this mean in our context? It means that there are no great heroes working with victims of prostitution and trafficking. There are only all-too-human, obedient, courageous followers of Jesus, who through His power bring freedom, deliverance, and new life. Ultimately, our treasure and their treasure is God—revealed to us all in His transforming glory!

> There are no great heroes working with victims of prostitution and trafficking. There are only all-too-human, obedient, courageous followers of Jesus, who through His power bring freedom, deliverance, and new life.

Lastly, some of our mistakes in fulfilling God's vision through Project Rescue ministries are shared transparently so that readers who feel called to minister to sexually exploited women and children in their local city or beyond might gain from our struggles and avoid pitfalls. Here it goes!

ASSUMING EVERYONE IN SEXUAL SLAVERY WANTS TO LEAVE, OR ONCE OUT, WILL WANT TO STAY OUT

As difficult as it is for us to believe, some victims have been in slavery for so long that their fear of the unknown and resignation to the known wins out over a desire to escape. They have learned to navigate exploitation, chaos, and the constant daily adrenaline of the world of prostitution in order to survive. Sometimes the opportunity to leave and the process and place of healing is such a difficult shift that they decide to return to the world of exploitation they know. The bondage of sexual slavery is not just physical. It's mental, emotional, relational, and spiritual.

ASSUMING THERE ARE EXPERTS IN THIS FIELD

There are experts in *specific parts* of the field from whom we are grateful to learn. Some aspects of how sexual exploitation works, and understanding victims' needs, are amazingly universal. But other aspects are cultural and regional; therefore, each person has to learn the local cultural context in which they work in order to minister most effectively. No shortcuts there!

Also, it takes so many different kinds of skills to minister to victims' multifaceted needs that good team players are much more necessary than "experts" (see chapter 11, "The Mafia Gets It. Why Don't We?"). Lastly, traffickers keep changing their strategies as law enforcement and those in helping professions learn their tactics. It's a moving target. This requires constant willingness to re-adapt the ministry approach, and constant sensitivity to the Spirit who teaches and gives wisdom in how to modify and work more effectively. About the time workers think they've figured out how to do this, things change.

FAILURE TO HAVE A LONG-TERM STRATEGY

When we first received K. K. Devaraj's call for help and responded positively to go down this road, we were responding in the moment to what we sensed was God's heart and purpose. While it was the right thing to do, we didn't know the "right" way to do it (not unusual in first steps of pioneering new ministries). So we had to seek God desperately, and learn as we went. Our formal mission statement, value statements, and best-practice documents developed as we learned.

> It's impossible to get where you need to go long-term in ministry to exploited women and children if you don't know what the end needs to be.

In a sense, we had an excuse for not having a long-term strategy at first. But there is no excuse for not developing one as quickly as possible with prayer, research, and good collaboration. I wish we had done that sooner than we did. It's impossible to get where you need to go long-term in ministry to exploited women and children if you don't know what the end needs to be. An exit strategy is critical to successful re-integration of survivors back into their community and mainstream culture.

ASSUMING A SALARY CREATES A CALL

A salary can hire staff, but a salary does not create a call. *Only God calls.* In the day-to-day stresses, challenges, and battles of working with prostituted women and children, the difference between someone called of God to this ministry who receives a salary and a person doing the work because they get paid a salary becomes uncomfortably apparent over time. Helping seemingly ungrateful, angry, manipulative, and sometimes demonized women and children on their healing journey 24/7, while also battling the aggressive schemes of madams, pimps, and corrupt policemen, takes a divine call from God in order to love and last. There's not enough salary in the world to keep you going some days without knowing God has called you.

ASSUMING WE KNOW WHAT VICTIMS OF INJUSTICE NEED

When we began Project Rescue, we assumed prostituted women and children needed what we would need in their place. Therefore, that is what we thought we needed to provide. But we have never been in their shoes, so we really couldn't know what they needed. Again, some of their deepest needs for trustworthiness, compassion, basic care, safety, community, and vocational training for a future profession are the same conceptually from culture to culture, nation to nation, and city to city. But the ways those needs are met can look different in different places.

For example, when offering vocational training to formerly prostituted women, a common way to express Christ's compassion has traditionally been to donate sewing machines so they can learn to sew and begin their own small businesses. While this is a viable strategy for economic sustainability in some countries, the work of a seamstress is viewed as a low-class profession with little dignity or value in other countries. By asking what is needed and what would add value to rescued women's lives in the local culture, our compassionate help can be more strategic. On the other hand, by failing to inquire about what is needed in a specific context, we can inadvertently perpetuate a woman's low status and lack of dignity by assuming that what works well in one country will work in another.

BEING TOO QUICK TO TAKE ON FINANCIAL RESPONSIBILITY

It was not until a few years down the road with Project Rescue ministries that we began to appreciate the contributions of those who do community development (sounds very unspiritual, right?). The basic premise of community development is that every (yes, every) community has resources to give and invest, no matter how impoverished it may appear.[28] It was all too easy in the early years of the ministry to assume that a major part of the resources to develop the ministry had to come through foreign funding rather than exploring what kinds of resources might already be available in the local city, state, or nation. In some areas, we created unnecessary dependence on foreign funding when many local Christians, organizations, and agencies had much to give. Thankfully, our national colleagues in India were very resourceful and creative in

---

28 Our colleagues Ron Bueno, founder of Enlace in El Salvador, Dr. JoAnn Butrin of Assemblies of God World Missions International Ministries, and Cindy Hudlin, formerly with World Vision and Project Rescue, have been especially valuable friends in expanding our understanding of the critical role of the local community in compassion ministries.

their initiatives to seek local community help in development. But we are still finding our way out of early rushes to compassionate judgment on who could help best and fastest.

UNDERESTIMATING THE SPIRITUAL AND SYSTEMIC BATTLE FOR THE MOST VULNERABLE

I'll never forget the meeting with our American colleagues when David first presented the vision for Project Rescue. He shared with them the world in Bombay that Devaraj and his team had stumbled into, and how we believed God wanted us to engage with this horrific need and incredible opportunity to bring freedom to women and children. We prayed together and my husband asked our team if they had any wisdom. Most were gracious and encouraging, even if they indicated they already had too much on their plates and knew it wasn't for them to be involved.

But then a pivotal moment occurred when elder missionary statesman Andrew McCabe stood to speak. Brother Andrew had been raised by Scottish missionary parents in North India, on the Nepali border. After going back to Scotland for university, he had returned to North India as a missionary himself to work a lifetime among the people he loved. He was now in his seventies.

"Brother Grant, I feel I need to speak. I believe we need to do this. These girls and women are in God's heart. *But I feel like I need to warn us, that if we do, it may cost us everything.* In all my years living on this sub-continent, nothing is so close to the heart of hell as this evil! Whenever anyone has attempted to help victims of prostitution, all hell breaks loose. We will pay a price. But I believe we need to do it."

The room was sober. We prayed together and committed to the journey of what would soon become Project Rescue. But the story was only beginning. My husband immediately left the meeting to take our two young daughters and me to the airport to catch a flight to another city. As we were driving through the chaotic traffic of the city of five million people, I caught my breath in horror. A little girl of about three followed her older brother into the traffic immediately into the path of our oncoming van. The boy successfully rushed to make it across safely while the little girl kept pursuing, and our driver braked in panic. Unfortunately, the van was too heavy and the distance too short. The impact was sickening as the vehicle hit the small girl. Suddenly people began running toward our van, and I knew what was coming. In many countries where people do not feel justice is available to the poor, the poor take justice into their own hands. Frequently after a traffic accident, the vehicle is mobbed, its occupants beaten, and the vehicle may even be torched while the occupants die inside. Instinctively, I began to roll up the car windows, pushed our girls down onto the floorboard while I prayed the name of Jesus. I remember thinking, "This is it. It's over!" David had immediately gotten out of the car to go to the little girl. Then, it was as if someone stopped a video. People running toward us stopped where they were. Within seconds that seemed like forever, David got back in the car and motioned to the driver to go on.

"But, David, where's the little girl?" I asked.

He pointed. "That's her running across the street to meet her family. There's not a mark on her body, not a broken bone, nothing. She's perfectly fine. It's as if nothing even touched her."

> The battle
> against evil is
> great, but
> our God
> is greater.

An elderly Hindu man standing on the concrete median within a few feet of our vehicle as it hit the child said to my husband, "Sir, you have just seen God."

This was only twenty minutes after leaving the meeting in which we had committed to pursue ministry to sexually-enslaved women and children. And for twenty-four hours, the girls and I faced one threatening and bizarre event after another. But moment by moment, we called out to God together, and His powerful presence surrounded us. Before we finished that journey, I knew that if God didn't continue to intervene miraculously, we would never make it home. He did . . . and we did! But that first twenty-four hours put us on a spiritual alert that has continued for seventeen years. I learned (in case we had ever doubted it!) that we had a very real personal enemy who was out to destroy us if we challenged his dominion over prostituted women and children. But I became even more aware that we had a real and powerful God who was more than able to cancel the schemes of the enemy and protect those who are committed to obeying His call to His mission! Yes, the battle against evil is great, but our God is greater. He is still performing miracles on behalf of those who put their trust in Him.

PRACTICAL CONSIDERATIONS FOR DEVELOPING MINISTRY TO THOSE IN SEXUAL SLAVERY

With over thirty-seven years of cross-cultural ministry experience, my husband and I have learned, sometimes painfully, that developing ministry to victims of sex trafficking and slavery is the most challenging and spiritually intensive ministry we've ever undertaken. It's also been the most rewarding. Engaging in the battle against this most horrific form of human depravity brings one face-to-face with the worst side of man without God and with the destructive power of Satan. But engaging in the battle against sexual slavery in the courageous compassion of Christ also brings one face-to-face with the life-changing power of God's raw grace. We have experienced personally that the love of Jesus shines most vibrantly when shared in the darkest places.

> We have experienced personally that the love of Jesus shines most vibrantly when shared in the darkest of places.

But learning to engage Christ's love and compassionate mission practically within that very dark world for the sake of its victims is messy and stretching to say the least. Several important issues that must be navigated in developing a Christian ministry to victims of sex trafficking are highlighted here.

THEOLOGICAL ISSUES

There is no value-free social response to human need and injustice. Response to human need and injustice always reflects the values and worldview of the person responding. One's religious worldview (or lack thereof) and cultural values answer the foundational questions of who man is, where he is headed, what has gone wrong, and therefore, how it can and should be addressed. Secular humanists, atheists, Buddhists, and Muslims approach these questions from very different perspectives and therefore come to very different conclusions on how to respond.

Thus it should not be surprising, but assumed, that an initiative focused on the injustice of sexual slavery or trafficking and the restoration of its victims developed by a Christian organization or mission should be unashamedly grounded in Christian theology and consistent with biblical values. To ensure this, missiologist Bryant Myers stresses the necessity of ongoing theological reflection while developing and doing all compassion ministries. [29]

To illustrate, if one believes a loving God created each human life in His image with a divine purpose, and that it is His will for that life to be lived with dignity and wholeness, that shapes how one views and relates to exploited teenage girls in Moldova. In contrast, if one believes the gods are capricious in relating to human beings, that misfortune is payment for sins in a past life, and that there are many cycles of life yet to live, that creates a different perception of victims of trafficking and a different view of the responsibility of others to help them.

One of the greatest theological challenges for Western evangelical Christians working with women and girls in sexual slavery is our tradition of viewing salvation primarily as a decisive, momentary event. From our experience interacting with sexually exploited women, the decision to follow Jesus and to find freedom and healing is more often a journey leading to new life in Christ rather than a single moment of radical transformation. Along the journey of decisions responding to Jesus, in which layers of darkness began to be broken, there is a time where a full breakthrough of light and life appears. But the breakthrough into new life and

---

29 Bryant Myers, *Walking with the Poor: Principles and Practices of Transformational Development* (Maryknoll, NY: Orbis Books, 1999).

the visible Light in women's eyes usually comes after they have responded numerous times over a period of time to God's truth, powerful intercession, and delivering prayer.

This was something BTC founder K. K. Devaraj had to grapple with from the beginning of the red-light district ministry. It's heart-wrenching to pray with women in sexual bondage for God's healing and deliverance in one moment only to watch them go back into the night and the violence of the brothel in the next. We must remember that yes, they are literally slaves.

However, with time, K. K. Devaraj and his outreach team began to view the process toward spiritual and physical freedom much like the exodus of the Israelites from slavery in Egypt. Through the various aspects of the ministry contacts, girls in bondage received help to make spiritual, mental, emotional, and physical preparation for their personal exodus out of slavery. Sometimes the spiritual freedom comes before the physical freedom can be obtained; in other cases, physical freedom is negotiated first, and spiritual, emotional, and mental freedom follow as victims experience God's love and healing in the aftercare home. No matter the timing and order of events, Jesus is ultimately the only One who can and does bring total freedom and new life to those in such complete bondage. We His children are privileged to work with Him and walk with them on the miraculous, messy journey.

> No matter the timing and order of events, Jesus is ultimately the only One who can and does bring total freedom and new life to those in such complete bondage.

MISSIOLOGICAL ISSUES

Each Christian mission has a statement of purpose and a strategy for pursuing that purpose. As missionaries and national coworkers prayerfully consider responding to sexual injustice, one of their greatest challenges is to determine how the ministry will relate to the larger vision and ministries of the mission.

Because the need of women and children in sexual slavery is so emotionally gripping, followers of Jesus who consider getting involved face several temptations:

Responding Too Quickly to an Immediate Need Without Considering Long-Term Implications

- Is your immediate reaction best for the victim's well-being or is it about your own personal sense of mission, significance, and fulfillment?

- Are you and your church/mission willing and prepared to deal with the inevitable spiritual, medical, legal, and political issues?

- Is the initiative you envision consistent with the mission statement of your larger church, organization, or ministry?

Moving Individually or as a Church/Missionary Family Without Local/National Colleagues

It takes time to prepare the hearts and minds of local or national church and colleagues for co-ownership of the vision. The following questions can help to evaluate this area:

- Is the project going to be under the leadership and ownership of a missionary organization, NGO, or the national church? Who leads?

- Who has the potential and commitment to make your vision effective in the culture long-term?

Allowing Donors to Drive the Pace of Ministry Development

Development decisions should be based on readiness factors on the ground, rather than being driven by substantial donors.

- Are promises made to foreign donors, regarding what can be accomplished on anti-trafficking and aftercare projects in developing world countries, unrealistic or even impossible in terms of "how life works" in the local culture?

- Are qualified, committed potential workers in place to handle the intensive responsibilities of aftercare for each project *before* proceeding with development? It's a whole lot easier to start things than keep them going!

In the case of Project Rescue Southern Asia, our leadership expressed concern regarding every aspect of the developing ministry over the first several years. One of the greatest concerns was how it fit—if, in fact, it did fit—with the four foundational priorities of the parent mission's philosophy: reaching (evangelism), church planting, training (discipleship), and touching (compassion ministries). In actuality, with intense scrutiny and intentionality, Project Rescue's mission and that of its affiliated ministries incorporates all four missional priorities of AGWM in its work with victims of sexual slavery. No, it's not "out there on some compassion/social justice limb" competing with evangelism and discipleship. It is evangelism and discipleship, as well as training and compassion. These Great Commission dynamics are inextricably intertwined every day in Project Rescue-affiliated ministries because God's mission cannot be accomplished without them.

If the larger organizational mission's philosophy is biblical and sound, scrutiny to ensure that a pioneer project dealing with a complex and dangerous issue such as sex trafficking and its victims' needs is consistent with mission philosophy ultimately sharpens and strengthens the ministry focus and practice rather than stifles or hinders it. Challenging questions by respected spiritual leaders are our friends in the complexity of doing courageous compassionate ministry.

SPIRITUAL ISSUES

The toll on workers dealing with women and children who have experienced unimaginable acts of sexual perversion and violence is impossible to calculate. For those who care, it is painful to hear the victims' stories first-hand and to imagine how they have managed to survive. The emotional, mental and physical wounds of sexual exploitation, especially among children, are raw. Yet, grappling with these kinds of traumatic issues are all part of a day's work when caring for victims of sexual slavery.

The dimension of intervention and holistic care-giving that sets Christian organizations apart is the spiritual one. Spiritual issues can be the most difficult to understand, most resistant to treatment, and most challenging in complexity. Worse, for Western Christians whose theology may not have prepared them for the reality of evil spiritual power, what they face daily in working with victims may leave them reeling, overwhelmed, confused, and powerless in spite of their degree in social work, counseling, or theology.

In their excellent study, "Sexually Exploited Children: Working to Protect and Heal," Phyllis Kilbourne and Marjorie McDermid briefly describe some of the most prevalent forms of sexual slavery (i.e., pornography, commercial sex tourism) and others that are less prevalent but that have hidden implications for child victims and those who seek to help them heal. For example, in India, the tradition of selling twelve-year-old daughters to Hindu temples as temple prostitutes (*devadasi*) is believed to buy parents the blessing of the gods. In this ritual process, the spirit of a goddess is invited to inhabit the young girl. Generally, this is the beginning not only of a life of sexual slavery and of sexually transmitted diseases, but of violent spiritual power beyond the child's control. The *devadasi* initiation is the fate of an estimated five to ten thousand young Indian girls a year.[30] Those who would help them must be as spiritually prepared as possible to deal with those kinds of destructive spiritual dynamics.

These kinds of ritual experiences and other forms of ritual sexual abuse common in Africa, Asia, and the Caribbean require a heightened sense of spiritual discernment and authority on the part of ministry workers. This is especially stretching for American and European workers ministering to women who have been trafficked into their own nations from nations where

---

30 Kilbourn and McDermid, 11.

ritual abuse is common. The trauma of ritual sexual abuse can lead to psychological disorders, such as dissociative disorder, and/or demonic spiritual bondage.[31] The behavioral symptoms can be so similar that caregivers need heightened spiritual sensitivity and training to differentiate between the two.

A word of caution is needed here for would-be caregivers. Sometimes those most drawn to the issue of sex trafficking and the needs of victims are those who have themselves been victims of some form of sexual abuse (i.e., child sexual exploitation, domestic sexual violence, rape, or prostitution). Former victims can become wonderful healers and caregivers—if and only if they have also experienced a level of deep healing of their own trauma over time. Helping victims of sexual slavery find healing is not a means for other victims to find their own personal healing. Until victimized individuals themselves have come to a place of healing and strength, exposure to those newly struggling from sexual trauma and to the destructive spiritual dynamics of the community of exploitation only serves to reawaken unhealed memories of trauma and abuse in caregivers. God can use you to powerfully help others on their journey to freedom, but first take time to find your own healing through Jesus and His followers who are trained to help. Let

> Former victims can become wonderful healers and caregivers—if and only if they have also experienced a level of deep healing of their own trauma over time.

---

31 Grant and Hudlin, 203.

them confirm when you are strong enough to serve. The sexually exploited in our world desperately need healthy healers!

PROMOTIONAL, DIGNITY, AND SECURITY ISSUES

Any nonprofit ministry or organization needs funding and some form of marketing in order to survive. Fortunately for Christian missions and affiliated ministries, the community of faith is generous by nature and touched by human need. The issue of human trafficking and its young victims is particularly abhorrent and intolerable to people of faith, and women are especially motivated to act. Having said that, well-educated and technology-savvy twenty-first-century donors tend to expect certain kinds of communication and promotional information from ministries they support. The first question Project Rescue representatives receive from interested persons and potential donors is, "Where is your website?" A Project Rescue website was launched during the second year of the ministry, but had to be discontinued. Because of the sensitivity required to protect the rescued women and girls and the national workers in the red-light districts from other predators, we were advised not to use their photos. When promoting the various aspects of the ministry, we could not use names of locations in Southern Asia for fear of retaliation by organized crime. Basically, for Project Rescue's first seven years in existence, there was more that we could not afford to share than we could share. A website was launched again after seven years of ministry, but only after careful evaluation of the risk involved and assurance that we could creatively minimize any risk to women and children on the healing journey while telling God's story of love and redemption.

This very real problem of would-be-helpers hurting became tragically clear after a young film director visited the Sonagachie red-light district in Kolkota, India. Zana Brisky was so genuinely moved by the plight of the prostituted women's children that she produced the Oscar-winning documentary, "Born Into Brothels," in 2005 to focus international awareness. It was very well done and gave a moving and accurate portrayal of the energetic, creative, beautiful children growing up in India's brothels.

Unfortunately, the world release of the much-heralded film and the resulting media attention placed the Sonagachie mothers and children in immediate danger of harassment, further stigmatization, and even heightened sexual violence. One of the young photographers featured in the film who had been in the process of restoration through a ministry in the district came to our colleague Joni Middleton in distress. "But, Auntie, what are people in America thinking about me?" she pleaded. As a result of the backlash against the film in Sonagachie district, many of the children could not return to school because their identities and background had been disclosed. One of the young girls featured was later targeted by police for sexual violence because she had become a celebrity, and raping her would be a prize. Another used her visibility over the years to become a "high class madam," an exploiter of younger prostituted girls. Tragically, without an understanding of the complex dynamics of global sex trafficking, well-meaning media attention simply makes children easier to find for sex tourists, pedophiles, and traffickers. Our good intentions—especially if uninformed—are not enough.

Child-sponsorship programs in the United States and Europe have conditioned donors to expect photos and letters from sponsored children. But as one of our colleagues stated in reaction to the inadvertent disregard for children's protection in the "Born into Brothels" project, "The children's safety is worth more than a photo." All of us who passionately want to help must re-think promotional strategies and the expectations of donors, whose funding is necessary to our work. We must involve the global church without jeopardizing the very women and children we are trying to help. In the epic battle to rescue exploited women and end sexual slavery, more publicity is not always better.

> Survivors need—no, deserve—dignity and privacy in their healing process.

The next question good people ask David and me is frequently, "When can we go see it?" In an increasingly mobile world, Western donors to compassion ministries assume they can go see whatever they help support. This has created an increasingly growing tension between donors' desires, demands, and the well-being and dignity of trafficking survivors in healing aftercare programs. As thousands of generous followers of Jesus demonstrate caring, Christ-like compassion by giving to help ministries to victims internationally, thousands of donors want to "go and see." With the best of intentions, the "just go-and-see" trend can inadvertently make unhealthy differences in traumatized girls and women's lives— differences that the caring givers and goers never intended.

Prostituted women and children have experienced years of unknown men coming by them on the streets to gawk. Now do visitors come by the hundreds to look at them in ministry aftercare homes? If they do not know visitors personally, are we re-exploiting in a different way? As my husband responded once in frustration to a persistent American pastor insistent on going to see girls in the aftercare homes because he had given some money, "These girls are not monkeys in the zoo!" (Yes, even ministers can get frustrated!)

Survivors need—no, deserve—dignity and privacy in their healing process. If my daughter had been brutally raped daily as a child and I had finally found a place for her to begin healing for her trauma, would I want strangers walking through her bedroom every week looking at her? Even if the strangers are generous and kind, it doesn't change the fact that a survivor's personal shame, hurt, and healing journey is being exposed to strangers.

It's time to ask if our condition for helping is actually hurting. Building projects don't have shame, trauma, and raw pain. Buildings are fairly easy to "go and see." But women and children coming out of sex slavery have all of these difficulties to extreme levels. Shouldn't our "go-and-see" approach be questioned for their sakes?

Good programs working with prostituted women and children protect them. They don't re-exploit them to raise funds. Their reluctance to have guests visit the women and children being restored should not be interpreted in a negative light. Their first priority is what's best for the recovering victims who desperately need the privacy and dignity so necessary to their trust and healing process.

In addition, there are the missionaries' and national workers' own security issues to be considered. Becoming actively involved in the fight against sexual slavery and in aftercare is a costly enterprise for missionaries. The costs are high financially, physically, emotionally, and spiritually. When someone challenges sexual slavery, he or she is challenging the darkest form of evil. Followers of Jesus must do so knowing that their engagement in this battle may cost them everything—including the privilege of continuing to serve in the country of their calling.

CONCLUSION

Is engaging in the battle against sexual trafficking and ministering to victims of sexual slavery around our world a good idea? No, not really. It is the most challenging compassionate ministry journey one could ever undertake on the most vile front in the epic battle between good and evil. It's not a "great idea."

But it is the heart of our just God. Isaiah's prophetic words foretell the bold ministry of Christ, the Anointed One, who would come to earth to bring good news, healing, and liberty to the poor, the broken-hearted, and those in bondage. The prophetic words soar with special meaning and promise for those devastated by sexual injustice and those divinely called to minister Christ's redeeming love to them.

> The Spirit of the LORD is upon Me . . . to comfort all who mourn, and provide for those who grieve in Zion— to bestow on them a crown of beauty instead of ashes, the oil of joy instead of mourning, and a garment of praise instead of a spirit of despair. They will be called oaks of righteousness, a planting of the LORD for the display of His splendor. They will rebuild the ancient ruins, and restore places long devastated; they will renew the ruined cities that have been devastated for generations. . . . Instead of your shame you will receive a double portion, and instead of disgrace you will rejoice in your inheritance. And so you will inherit a double portion in your land, and everlasting joy shall be yours. For I, the LORD, love justice.
> (Isaiah 61:1–8)

SUGGESTED LEARNING EXPERIENCE

The story of Project Rescue's journey as a ministry raises questions that inevitably need to be addressed when we, as people of faith, commence working with prostituted women and children. In your small group or class, tackle the following discussion questions to deepen your insight into the integration of this kind of compassionate initiative from a biblical perspective. Which were the most pressing questions that came to your mind as you read the chapter? Why?

1. Were any of your personal assumptions (stereotypes) about ministry to trafficked and exploited women and children challenged? Identify them and describe in what ways your understanding was stretched.

2. How would and could such a ministry look in your city? Discuss the following aspects that would need to be addressed:

   • Is your local church prepared to do such a ministry and receive victims of sexual exploitation in all its forms? If not, what could be your next steps toward that goal?

   • What are the security issues locally?

   • What resources already exist (both human and economic) in the community that could be mobilized for this initiative?

   • What kinds of relationships are you willing to develop with those in great darkness for the sake of fulfilling Christ's mandate? Identify the potential costs and risks of building those kinds of relationships.

3. Are you one who assumes that if you give you have a right to "go and see" where your money is being spent? Discuss the possible tensions between donors' desires and the privacy and dignity of victims of sexual injustice. What are some possible ways those tensions can be resolved with integrity—both for donors and those who are being blessed by their help?

4. What are the differences between a good secular organization working to help provide care for trafficked women and children and a good faith-based organization based on the person and message of Jesus Christ?

Finish the session with focused prayer for wisdom and God's direction. What is He calling you to do, both personally and as a group? How can this call fulfill His mission to bring freedom to captives: body, mind, and spirit?

FOR FURTHER STUDY

- David and Beth Grant. *Beyond the Shame: Project Rescue's Fight to Restore Dignity to Survivors of Sexual Slavery*. Springfield, MO: Onward Books, 2013.

CHAPTER 5

WHERE IS TRUTH?: LIMPING ON THE ROAD TO FREEDOM

If you hold to my teaching, you are really my disciples. Then
you will know the truth, and the truth will set you free.
JOHN 8:31–32

From whence comes the voice that can challenge this
culture on its own terms, a voice that speaks its own
language and yet confronts it with the authentic figure
of the crucified and living Christ so that it is stopped in
its tracks and turned back from the way of death?[32]
LESSLIE NEWBIGIN

A class of students in a Christian university was discussing contemporary global issues, in particular, poverty and the responsibility of followers of Jesus to the poor. After some time, an young American man who had been raised in Africa of missionary parents jumped into the dialogue: "I just want to go back to Africa and feed children who are poor. There have been way too many words, too much preaching. If we will just feed the poor, they will see Jesus!"

---

32 Lesslie Newbigin (1986). *Foolishness to the Greeks: The Gospel and Western Culture* (Grand Rapids, MI: Eerdmans, 1986), 9.

A number of his classmates immediately agreed. Another student quoted the famous words attributed to St. Francis of Asissi, "Speak the gospel [truth] at all times—and when necessary use words."[33]

But will the sincerely shared food for the hungry or cup of cold water given by followers of Jesus be interpreted by those who receive it in the way it is perceived by the person giving it—in a way that causes the recipient to see Jesus—without spoken truth? It's human nature that the things heard, seen, and experienced are interpreted through a personal historical, cultural, and religious lens. So, in reality, a gift or benevolent action received is interpreted in light of factors such as:

- who is giving it
- the giver's and receiver's respective cultural backgrounds
- how it relates historically to the recipient's cultural background, if different, i.e., if one culture was historically dominated by the other as a colony or if the two cultures represented by giver and receiver have been at war
- the recipient's religious worldview
- if non-Christian, whether Christianity is viewed in a positive light or in a negative light—and if viewed suspiciously as being manipulative for conversionary purposes

---

33 Quoted by Philip W. Eaton, *Engaging the Culture, Changing the World* (Downers Grove, IL: InterVarsity Press, 2011), 121.

Admittedly, there are reasons for contemporary Christians to gravitate to the St. Francis-attributed approach. In an internet-dominated, media-saturated world of words, including "Christian" ones, filling the air and cyberspace round the clock, one can turn in exasperation from the noise to the simplicity of silent action—action hopefully so compelling and powerful that it makes words unnecessary. Yes, there are far too many religious words. But in the biblically sound re-engagement of evangelical Christians with justice and compassionate action toward human need in our world, are we leaving something critical behind? In the twenty-first-century response of followers of Jesus to the hungry, the diseased, the enslaved, and the exploited, *where is truth?*

Western culture at large has become casual, relativistic, and adaptive about truth. The "truth," as presented in the worlds of media, politics, and the courtroom, is disconcertedly determined by the personal or corporate agenda of the person presenting it. That is the world in which the Missouri exploiters of the enslaved young woman dared to think they would be cleared of any wrongdoing; if they could make a case that the young victim actually "liked" the attention, they hoped to be cleared of exploitation charges. The headline news on any given day is full of competing accounts of "truth." In that kind of murky world where injustice occurs, it is perhaps easier to recognize the lies in order to recognize the essentiality of God's truth.

The lies of those who enslave, abuse, violate, and betray are tragically predictable and have changed little through history. They are similar in any language—from the streets of Amsterdam to Bangkok to the bedrooms of New York City. That fact in itself points to the existence of an Evil One who is the Father of All Lies. Sometimes, the lies of abusers and perpetrators of exploitation are spoken, sometimes unspoken; but they are always insidiously communicated. The vernacular and idioms change from decade to decade, but the lies are eerily the same:

> *"You are trash!"*
> *"You will always be trash."*
> *"You are worthless! Nobody wants you."*
> *"I'll take care of you. Nobody understands you, but I do."*
> *"You are hopeless! You deserve to be treated like this!"*
> *"It's useless to try to escape. No one will believe you."*
> *"You were born trash. You will die trash."*
> *"I love you."*

THE TRUTH ABOUT TINA

At twelve years of age, Tina disappeared somewhere into the dark world of India's red-light districts. Born to a prostituted woman in brothels identified by numbers, the young girl was identified by women and madams alike as one who most urgently needed safe shelter. She was sweet, quiet, and growing into a beautiful young woman. So when a Christian group home was found, Tina's mother agreed to let her leave in spite of the daily threats and violence by her pimp husband. The last thing this "father" wanted was to see this young girl's profitability in the business lost to him.

Unfortunately, because the other girls in the shelter were from other backgrounds, Tina did not fit in. After several weeks of what the director described as destructive behavior, Tina's father was called to come take her "home." And to the heart-sickening horror of the staff who had been working prayerfully in the red-light district to see Tina find safety, healing, and a new life, the young girl disappeared back into the world of darkness with the very man who intended to keep her there.

But in God's mysterious ways of redeeming events as well as people, this tragedy became a catalyst for action. People of faith in the local church and outreach ministries realized the time had come to start an aftercare and prevention home specifically for young girls like Tina who were being born into the city's brothels. Serious, intentional collaboration began with national and foreign followers of Jesus to make this happen. Within several months, a home was found, and the first little girls came to live at the request of their mothers—from the same red-light district where Tina had lived. Within weeks, the girls were blossoming, attending school, and for the first time in their lives, learning who Jesus was and how to worship Him. With loving, wise, spiritually sensitive care, they were finding freedom from the destructive demonic powers so prevalent in the world of sexual slavery.

Then one day, a call came from outreach workers in the red-light district. A young woman of about twelve years of age had been discovered by some of their team members, and her father and mother said she could leave. She needed a home—but could the new shelter take her? The director and staff quickly went to work getting another bed ready for this young girl. When the car pulled up to the home, to their joy, it was Tina—but not the same Tina as before. The Tina we had known before was demure, sweet, a child. The young girl who stepped out of the car was a woman—face dark, eyes downcast, and dressed like an adult. Someone, something, had died.

In the difficult weeks that followed, the dedicated staff began the challenging work of healing, trauma counseling, medical care, and spiritual warfare for a young girl's soul. And they heard all the lies of a victim about her abuser . . . words that the other younger daughters of prostituted mothers living in the home with Tina now recognized as false.

> *"I want to go back to my 'father.' He loves me!"*
> *"My 'father' is good to me! He gives me things."*
> *"I'm special to my 'father.' You don't understand!"*
> *"He treats me like a woman! He loves me."*

Thankfully, those working with Tina, like others working to bring justice and healing, have learned the critical and essential power of God's truth in liberating and transforming care. In response to the lies of Satan that Tina, her mom, and thousands of other women and girls hear every day in exploitation, her new family and friends began to speak affirming words of life-giving truth into this young girl's life:

> *"You are special because you have been created by God, your heavenly Father, for a good purpose!"*
> *"You have a heavenly Father who loves you, created you, and gave you life."*
> *"You have God-given gifts to use and celebrate. God will use you to bless others as others are using their God-given gifts to bless you!"*
> *"You can trust your heavenly Father. He is good, He is trustworthy, and He has good plans for your life. He will never betray you!"*
> *"When we give our lives to Jesus, He makes us new girls and women. He gives us His identity as His children."*
> *"Through loving and serving Jesus, you will become the strong woman of God He created you to be."*

For a couple of years, Tina learned God's truth and grew in her sense of God-given value and dignity. Her education, medical care, and participation in a local church were all critical components of providing new life and a future to this young girl born in a brothel. But it is the spoken and lived-out truth of God's Word, woven like a

> In the journey of freedom from slavery, lies, and exploitation, God's eternal truth cannot be overlooked, compromised, or neglected in the process.

beautiful thread through Tina's days, that gave her spiritual, mental, and emotional hope and freedom. This doesn't mean that healing was easy or will be easy in the future. There have been difficult days when the darkness of her memories intrude and threaten to dominate again. Most difficult are times of visiting "home," as Tina's father attempts to re-exploit the sexual vulnerability of a young girl.

In the journey of freedom from slavery, lies, and exploitation, God's eternal truth cannot be overlooked, compromised, or neglected in the process. Without God's truth, in spite of the best intentions, our attempts at social justice for the "Tinas" in our world are only temporary detours, a time-out from exploitation, and unfulfilled promises on their journey of slavery. Physical rescue from a brothel does not in and of itself provide the mental, emotional, and spiritual transformation necessary for a different future for those in contemporary captivity. Followers of Jesus who are committed to engagement in our world's most pressing needs cannot separate God's justice from God's eternal truth. If we try, it will be the lies of a boyfriend, an abusing husband, a pimp, a pedophile, or the Evil One against our own human opinions and words. But when just actions and God's truth are engaged together, they are supernaturally liberating—just as the One who is truth proclaimed they would be (John 14:6).

YOUR TRUTH, MY TRUTH, OR GOD'S TRUTH?

The Word of God provides insights into the exclusive and essential power of God's eternal truth.

- *Truth, the protector from sin:* Psalm 119:11, "I have hidden your word in my heart, that I might not sin against you."

- *Truth, the illuminator of direction and guidance:* Psalm 119:105, "Your word is a lamp for my feet, a light on my path."

- *Truth, the eternal and unchanging:* Isaiah 40:8, "The grass withers and the flowers fall, but the word of our God endures forever."

- *Truth, Creator and One with God:* John 1:1–3, "In the beginning was the Word, and the Word was with God, and the Word was God. He was with God in the beginning. Through him all things were made; without him nothing was made that has been made."

- *Truth, the Incarnate Christ:* John 1:14, "The Word became flesh and made his dwelling among us. We have seen his glory, the glory of the one and only Son, who came from the Father, full of grace and truth."

- *Truth, the only Way:* John 14:6, "Jesus answered, 'I am the way and the truth and the life. No one comes to the Father except through me."

- *Truth revealed through the Spirit of truth:* John 16:13, "But when he, the Spirit of truth, comes, he will guide you into all truth."

- *Truth as armor of God against the Evil One's schemes:* Ephesians 6:11, 13, 14, 17, "Put on the full armor of God, so that you can take your stand against the devil's schemes. . . . Therefore put on the full armor of God, so that when the day of evil comes, you may be able to stand your ground, and after you have done everything, to stand. Stand firm, then, with the belt of truth buckled around your waist. . . . Take the helmet of salvation and the sword of the spirit, which is the word of God."

- *Truth as catalyst for repentance and escape from bondage:* 2 Timothy 2:24–26, "And the Lord's servant must not be quarrelsome but must be kind to everyone, able to teach, not resentful. Opponents must be gently instructed, in the hope that God will grant them repentance leading them to a knowledge of the truth, and that they will come to their senses and escape from the trap of the devil, who has taken them captive to do his will."

- *Truth alive, powerful, and discerning:* Hebrews 4:12, "For the word of God is alive and active. Sharper than any double-edged sword, it penetrates even to

dividing soul and spirit, joints and marrow; it judges
the thoughts and attitudes of the heart."

When reviewing these key Scriptures regarding God's Word
and truth, at the heart is the person of Jesus, the One sent by God to
be truth incarnate. All the Old Testament leads up to the coming of
the promised Messiah—Jesus, the One through whom salvation and
deliverance would come. The New Testament tells of Jesus' coming in
flesh as the truth; His crucifixion as atonement for sin; and the One
in whom the promise of salvation, healing, and deliverance has and
will be fulfilled. The Word of God—His truth revealed in Christ—
is at the heart and foundation of
our faith and hope for ourselves
and all humanity. In a world of
injustice perpetuated with lies,
not just any "truth" will do.

> In a world of injustice perpetuated with lies, not just any "truth" will do. God's truth alone is inherently life-changing.

God's truth alone is
inherently life-changing. But
it must be made known to
men, women, boys, and girls in
need if it is to transform. Faith
in God and His Word comes by hearing it. How can the broken,
addicted, poor, and enslaved believe in hope if they do not hear
about the only One who gives miraculous transformational hope?
In some form, the message of Christ and God's truth about Him
must be shared—whether in a slum street, a house church, a small
group, a Starbucks round table, or prison cell, this message of
Christ is ordained of God, anointed by the Spirit, and confirmed
miraculously by God's supernatural power. Whether preached
enthusiastically to a crowd from a platform as it is by my husband,

or shared quietly, personally and informally as it is by myself one-on-one with a woman escaping sexual violence, the good news of Jesus Christ and His promises has power to touch and change lives.

Perhaps this sounds like religious theory or dogma. But as my husband and I have traveled to over thirty countries and shared Christ and His message of hope and salvation in amazingly diverse settings to people of many cultures, from the richest to the poorest, I've been amazed to witness the power of the gospel at work. God's grace really is amazing!

LIFE IS BLACK AND WHITE, AND ALL YOU NEED IS JESUS

But God's truth must be shared with integrity and wisdom. Kristy Childs of Kansas City, Missouri, is an activist. In her early teens, she was trafficked and ended up spending over a decade of her life in sexual exploitation. As a survivor who received help and healing in her thirties, Kristy founded Veronica's Voice, a nationally-recognized, multifaceted, nonprofit organization dedicated to sex trafficking awareness, demand reduction, and providing critically needed services for survivors.[34] It was on her own journey from slavery to healing that Kristy developed a relationship with God and His power to change lives.

But as someone who experienced the horrors of exploitation and is working constantly to help other victims, Kristy has concerns about people of faith who want to engage in this issue and work with survivors. As a woman who knows this dark world from both sides, she offers some serious cautions for followers of Jesus:[35]

34 See www.veronicasvoice.org.

35 Taken from personal conversations, August 2011.

1. Don't make promises to victims you cannot keep.
   They have already heard too many promises that
   have never been kept.

2. Don't make promises for God and His Word that He
   did not make. To do so is spiritually and relationally
   reckless and undermines the victim's potential
   journey of faith in God and confidence in His
   Word. Some of us remember the song, "Something
   Beautiful, Something Good" made popular in the
   American evangelical church during the 1960s and
   1970s. In one of my husband's meetings in India, I
   began to sing by request the promises encouraging
   those listening—largely poor—that if they gave
   their lives to Jesus, He would "make something
   beautiful" out of their lives. Suddenly, I realized
   that their decision to follow Jesus could cost them
   everything, including their lives, and that for many of
   them it would certainly include persecution. Is that
   "something beautiful"? God is good on *His* promises,
   but not necessarily on ours.

3. While prayer and intercession are desperately
   needed, keep it personal and private until trust is
   established on some level with the victim and prayer
   is requested. Again, as in spoken truth, imposed
   prayer can undermine a future relationship where
   God's help will be welcome. Victims of injustice
   and exploitation too easily judge God and His
   trustworthiness—for good or bad— based on the
   perceived sensitivity or insensitivity of the person
   coming to help them "in Jesus' name."

In *Prophetic Dialogue: Reflections on Christian Mission Today*, Bevans and Schroeder commend missologist David Bosch's concept of "bold humility." Bosch exhorts contemporary Christians engaged in mission to boldly proclaim the truth of the gospel like God does: "with patience, respect, and in dialogue." [36]

> Victims of injustice and exploitation too easily judge God and His trustworthiness— for good or bad— based on the perceived sensitivity or insensitivity of the person coming to help them "in Jesus' name."

Kristy Child's concerns are honest and perhaps a little painful for followers of Jesus who are full of compassion and genuinely motivated to help hurting people. Bosch's approach may be less to our liking than breaking down brothel doors. But if God has actually called us to preach good news to the poor, proclaim freedom for prisoners, and recovery of sight for the blind, ensuring we do so with authenticity, integrity, and wisdom is not optional. It's absolutely essential.

CONFRONTED WITH TRUTH AT THE VILLAGE WELL

She was obviously not the most respected woman in the village. That would be understandable. Her personal life was complicated and messy and definitely set her apart from good moral women. In a

---

36 Stephen B. Bevans, and Roger P. Schroeder, *Prophetic Dialogue: Reflections on Christian Mission Today* (Maryknoll, NY: Orbis Books, 2011), 61.

culture that valued community, she found herself alone. Alone, that is, until she went to the well to draw water and met a man.

This was a different man. The woman had definitely known a few men—in fact too many men for her conservative culture—and that was part of her problem. But this man was a Jew who would naturally despise her and her people. So between her gender and her ethnic background, He should have had nothing to do with her. To her amazement, though, He asked her for help, and the conversation began.

By the side of a Middle Eastern well, this Jew offered the Samaritan woman several unexpected and seemingly undeserved gifts: dignity as a person, disarming prophetic but nonjudgmental honesty about her past, and a personal revelation of who He was in spite of it all. And her encounter with Truth incarnate was so liberating that she had the courage to return to her village and unashamedly share with her community that she had met the Christ. This woman was no longer crippled by her wounded past. Her shame was cancelled and her bondage shattered (John 4:4–28). The One who is truth had set her free!

CONCLUSION

QUESTIONS FOR COMPASSIONATE ENGAGEMENT

Using the following chart (Common Myths That Fuel Injustice) as a guide for reflection and dialogue. Discuss the reality and legitimacy of common cultural myths that inadvertently encourage injustice and exploitation. Are they true? Discuss why or why not.

Analyze each myth against the framework of truth as communicated by God in Scripture. Identify the correlating

Scripture truth and its practical and spiritual implications for followers of Jesus in the twenty-first century.

COMMON MYTHS THAT FUEL INJUSTICE

MYTHS (Source: Culture)	GOD'S TRUTH (Source: Scripture)
Some people were born poor and will always be poor.	
Some girls are just born promiscuous and will always be promiscuous.	
Gay men deserve AID's and get what they deserve.	
Rape usually occurs because women are promiscuous.	
In most cases, prostitution is something women choose because they are bad women.	
Once a girl or woman is raped, she's "damaged goods". No one would want her.	
Pornography is a victimless crime. Even children filmed for porn get paid for it.	
If prostitutes really wanted to get out, they could. It's their choice.	
If people immigrate to a country illegally, they deserve to be exploited.	

SUGGESTED LEARNING EXPERIENCE

Revisiting the account of the woman at the well narrated in John 4, consider together the role of Jesus and His revelation of truth to the woman in this spiritual encounter.

1. What impact did this encounter have on the woman spiritually? Socially? Emotionally? Relationally?

2. Suggest how the disciples would have responded to the woman had Jesus not been there, and why.

3. Who are some groups of women in your city, community, and/or church whose life experiences would be comparable to the woman at the well?

4. Do you or your church in any way relate to such women? If so, how? What do you bring to them in Jesus' name on their journey? What fears would you have to face in order to walk the healing journey with them?

5. Pray together for wisdom in how to engage the broken and wounded in your community both in action and in liberating truth.

FOR FURTHER STUDY

- Haugen, Gary A. *Just Courage: God's Great Expedition for the Restless Christian*. Downers Grove, IL: InterVarsity Press, 2008.

- Litfin, D. "Works and Words: Why You Can't Preach the Gospel with Deeds—And Why It's Important to Say So." *Christianity Today* 56 no. 5 (May 2012): 40–43.

- Sheikh, Bilquis. *I Dared to Call Him Father*. 7th ed. Grand Rapids, MI: Chosen Books, 2009.

CHAPTER 6

TAKING OFF THE STERILE GLOVES

Jesus went through all the towns and villages, teaching in their
synagogues, proclaiming the good news of the kingdom,
and healing every disease and sickness. When he saw the
crowds, he had compassion on them, because they were
harassed and helpless, like sheep without a shepherd.

MATTHEW 9:35-36

After a long sweltering day in Kolkata, our daughter Jennifer
returned from volunteering at Mother Teresa's Home for the
Destitute and Dying. A nursing student, she wanted to spend some
of her summer putting her skills to work where help is desperately
needed. Going back to Kolkata was like a second home, full of
wonderful memories with founders Dr. Mark and Huldah Buntain,
and many other dear family friends in the Kolkata Assemblies of
God Mission. But for the first time she was returning as a young
adult to take first steps in ministry as a nurse.

"Mom, I had to make a decision today." Soberly, our daughter
began to describe walking between women at Mother Teresa's
Home—impoverished women lying on pallets on the floor who
had been brought there to die with some sense of dignity and
compassion. Her responsibility, between helping feed those who

could eat and bathing parched bodies, was to keep the women as comfortable as possible during their final days of life. As Jennifer walked between the women, some would grasp for her long skirts as she walked by. For an American college student with a strong sense of personal private space, her intuitive response was to recoil. But wait, why was she here? Jennifer determined that when she could, she would stop, kneel down beside those who reached for her, and try to respond, despite the fact that her ability to understand and connect was definitely limited since she did not speak their local language.

But as Jennifer knelt down beside a dying woman in the slums of Kolkata for the first time, the woman clutched her hand and pulled it desperately to her parched cheek. Suddenly, this young nursing student realized that at the end of this woman's life, her greatest hunger was for someone to touch her . . . with kindness, comfort, and dignity. Tragically, everything about this woman created by God would have kept people in her culture from doing just that. She was a woman, but not only that; she was a poor woman, and now a diseased and dying woman. If she had been touched at all before coming to die at Mother Teresa's Home, it very likely would not have been with compassion.

Suddenly, Jennifer caught her breath. Part of her good nursing education in America was to place a high priority on creating a sterile environment for both nurse and patient. So like all the American nursing students who had come, our daughter had packed her sterile gloves. And of all the places one would need them most, it would certainly be in a place of death and disease. But as the woman pulled our daughter's hand to her face for comfort, Jennifer experienced a defining moment. Would she leave on her safe, sterile gloves that put a cold, secure distance between herself and this woman—definitely the "professional" thing to do—or would she take them off to allow her hand to touch the face of the woman so starved for caring human contact?

"Mom, how could I touch her face with sterile gloves? I couldn't do it. I've put my gloves in the suitcase, and I'll just have to trust God."

From the beginning of creation's story in Genesis, we see a God who chose to come close to His creation and take off the sterile gloves. Even after Adam and Eve sinned in the garden of Eden, God came looking for them when they hid (Gen. 3:8–9). Sadly, after the fall, this closeness was damaged by sin; nonetheless the grand theme of God's history with man is finding a way to restore the relationship and come close. Through the institution and fulfillment of sacrificial offerings in the Old Testament and through God giving His Son, Jesus, sacrificially in the New Testament, God's ultimate intention has always been to bring men and women out of the bondage of sin and into relationship, intimately close to Himself as sons and daughters.

God's continual desire for proximity and closing the distance are most meaningfully revealed in the way He sent Jesus, Immanuel (a name that means God with us). Jesus'

> From the beginning of creation's story in Genesis, we see a God who chose to come close to His creation and take off the sterile gloves.

coming was not a virtual intervention, live-streamed from the safety of heaven into humanity's messy world (ask Mary!) It was dirty, painful, sweaty, "low-class," and shameful (where were Mary's parents?). Jesus was sent from His Father in heaven to practice what we refer to in missions as "total immersion with a people": knowing their pride, their weaknesses, their joys, and their anguish. This was also an immersion in a place, in a culture, in a community, and in time. Ask the woman who had suffered with bleeding for twelve years (Matt. 9:20–22). Her story underlines Jesus' compassion—a compassion so great that He did not withhold Himself from being touched or from touching those in need (Matt. 14:35–36).

STERILE GLOVES COMPASSION: A CRIPPLED, SANITIZED JESUS

Let's think about how we personally "do" compassion as individual followers of Jesus and as the community of faith. If people in our local communities can only see Jesus through observing us, His people, what kind of Jesus do they see?

- *A Jesus without feet*—because we His children won't walk the distance to those in need?

- *A Jesus without sight*—because we His people close our eyes and refuse to see the people in need around us?

- *A Jesus without a voice*—because we His people are reluctant or afraid to use the voice He has given us?

- *A Jesus with a divided heart*—because we His people choose when to open or close our hearts and practice "selective compassion" as we lock people into social, cultural, economic, and religious categories?

- *A Jesus without hands*—because we His children hesitate to touch, feed, and heal those whom Jesus would touch, feed and heal?

We see this kind of crippled misrepresentation of Jesus by His disciples in spite of the fact that they had the advantage of literally watching and following Him. The Gospels describe awkward, uncomfortable contrasts between Jesus' compassion, which drove Him close to those in need irrespective of gender, age, social status, and religion, and the all-too-human-responses of His disciples—responses with which I can sadly identify. A few thought-provoking questions help uncover our own tendencies to practice "sterile-glove compassion."

- Would I have taken time to see children and include them in my busy day like Jesus did, or would I have brushed them off as distractions to our ministry? (Mark 10:13–16)

- Would I have stopped in the middle of a crowd of hundreds of people to acknowledge a woman suffering from bleeding, or would I have let it go as potentially embarrassing for all of us? (Mark 5:24–34)

- Would I have been sensitive to the fact that those who came to hear me teach had come a long way and were seriously hungry, or would I let the logistics of feeding them and my own focus on finishing my lectures discourage me from acting? After all, meals weren't included in the price of the conference! (Mark 8:1–8)

- Would I have had compassion on the soldier whose ear my dear friend misguidedly cut off trying to defend me, taking the time to stop and heal him, or

would I have left him earless and in pain because
he wasn't "one of us" and the situation was volatile?
(Luke 22:49–50)

REASONS FOR KEEPING OUR DISTANCE

In reflecting on our possible natural responses to these scenarios from Scripture, we can find more than enough so-called good reasons in the twenty-first century to keep the sterile gloves on. Choosing to come close to those in need and engage in holistic compassion is complicated. We cannot afford to be simplistic and naïve. All the following considerations can affect how and how much we decide to get close in compassionate outreach locally or globally as a church. All have some degree of legitimacy to consider.

PHYSICAL DANGERS

Violent gangs, dangerous wife abusers who resent those who help, drug lords protecting their turf, people under the influence of illegal drugs, struggling alcoholics, and demonic manifestations are only a few potential dangers that come to mind. The influence of the Evil One who seeks to destroy takes many forms.

Medical Factors

Those in bondage are frequently dealing with life-threatening medical issues, sometimes contagious, sometimes perceived as contagious (i.e., HIV/AIDS, sexually transmitted diseases, tuberculosis, leprosy).

Cultural Norms

Every culture, and to a lesser degree, every subculture, has its own definitions of what is considered appropriate proximity for family and close friends as compared to acquaintances and strangers. Norms regarding cross-gender space and communication are especially clearly defined and strongly held in traditional cultures. A cross-cultural minister who is either unaware of local gender-appropriate use of touch and space or chooses to ignore it does so at a cost.

LEGAL CONCERNS

The twenty-first-century world has become increasingly litigious, and this is especially so in the United States, where far too many people seem to be looking for a reason to bring a lawsuit. This tendency is heightened—with good reason—in areas where children are perceived as vulnerable to abuse, violence, or sexual exploitation. While the need for child protection is critical, this has also created an environment where even Jesus would have been suspect for inviting children into His world and heart. For churches and ministries around the world, the legal scrutiny, suspicion, and legislative codes surrounding ministry to children and/or minors can give serious hesitation to would-be visionaries.

SECURITY ISSUES

So many people in greatest need of Christ's compassion around the world fall prey to the control of organized crime, drug dealers, pimps, corrupt politicians, and gangs—to name a few. To try to bring life change to victims can bring danger not only to the victims, but to those who dare try to help them and change the status quo. In global missions in highly sensitive areas, working with some populations can actually cost the missionary his or her visa in that country. Not infrequently, there is a strong correlation between the economic profitability of a victimized population and the level of jeopardy to those who try to help them.

ECONOMIC REALITIES

Every compassionate initiative undertaken by a local church has a price tag. How much can we "afford" to give to those who may never give back—or never accept the Jesus we know and love? The economic bottom line is not only an indicator of a church's ability to engage in compassionate ministry, but of its motivation for doing so. Is a compassionate outreach only considered "strategic" and "worth it" if it translates into "souls"(decisions to follow Jesus)?

LACK OF SPIRITUAL READINESS

Compassion ministries can appear deceptively easy and spiritually nonthreatening to the uninitiated, because they often begin by addressing specific perceived physical needs (i.e., hunger, medical issues, or poverty). However, whenever believers take off the sterile gloves to address physical needs as commanded by Christ, they will inevitably bump into the rest of the person and potentially their community . . . emotionally, mentally, socially, and spiritually.[37] Coming close by meeting a physical need is only the proverbial

---

37 See chapter 12, "Supernatural Power for a Supernatural Compassion."

tip of the iceberg in life-changing compassion. And is it biblical, ethical, or missional to "touch and run"?

Fear of Exposing Personal Inadequacy

Perhaps as individual believers who desire to obey Christ's command to come close to those who suffer, no fear is more debilitating than the possibility of others realizing that we are inadequate. Like the reasons listed above, this fear definitely has grounds, because we are inadequate. Like Jesus' well-meaning disciples who tried to cast out a demon and failed miserably (Matt. 17:14–21), whenever we take steps of faith to bring healing and/or deliverance, we come uncomfortably face-to-face with ourselves as well as with the hurting. Any pretense of spirituality, self-confidence, and self-adequacy is easily shattered in a moment for all to see when we are face-to-face with a woman with no hope, it's 113 miserable degrees in a place of death and disease with no air-conditioning or amenities—and we have contracted parasites. We quickly see sides of ourselves we were never able to see before, when life was comfortable and convenient.

> Whenever believers take off the sterile gloves to address physical needs as commanded by Christ, they will inevitably bump into the rest of the person and potentially their community . . . emotionally, mentally, socially, and spiritually.

> Obediently coming
> close and touching
> people with Christ's
> healing, delivering,
> transforming power
> is intregal to who
> *He* is and what
> *He* came to do.

The good news—no, the life-changing news—about obeying Christ's commands and being led of the Holy Spirit in daring to reach out to those in need around us is that in doing so we also come face to face with Jesus! Why are we surprised that the One who came to seek and save hurting people and has called us to minister to them in His name is imminently there by His Spirit to empower us to do so when we obey? In those moments of His revelation, we are wonderfully relieved and reminded that Jesus-like compassion ministry really never is about us. Obediently coming close and touching people with Christ's healing, delivering, transforming power is integral to who *He* is and what *He* came to do.

REASONS FOR COMING CLOSE
TO THOSE IN NEED

There are compelling reasons for individual believers and the church to take off its sterile gloves and dare to come close to hurting people in courageous compassion.

- Jesus did it and requires it of His followers as well. At the most basic level of true Christianity, practicing compassion in many forms is commanded by God (Mic. 6:8, James 1:27).

- It provides people who don't know Christ or even who deny His reality a disarming, unexpected glimpse of our engaged Father God, who loves unconditionally and acts with genuine love through His children.

- The numbers of hurting people globally are staggering, and there is a disquieting realization among both secular and religious people that the situation for millions of people groups in our world is dismal at best, even hopeless. If the church who knows the One who is hope does not act, then who? If the church doesn't act now, then when?

- Taking off our sterile gloves with those in need lessens the possibility that our motives are not a reflection of God's heart and mission. Ministering close, one-on-one in compassion moves us from serving issues at a distance to knowing, loving, and serving real people Jesus loves up-close in life-changing ways.

JENNIFER: THE REST OF THE STORY

Our daughter, Jennifer, left her Kolkata summer internship as a nursing student with a much more realistic and nuanced understanding of what it means to serve the poor and dying. Taking off her sterile gloves became a fitting metaphor for her future work. After graduation, she became a nurse for the elderly in long-term care, helping them deal with their later days and dying. But she also left Kolkata with a serious case of parasites. Yes, taking off the gloves always has a price. But our call by Jesus to a courageous compassion deserves no less.

CONCLUSION

SUGGESTED LEARNING EXPERIENCE

Break into small groups and read together through "Maile's Story," one section at a time. After each section, discuss the reflection questions in your small group and debrief together at the end of the session.

MAILE'S STORY: THE WOMAN LIVING UNDER THE BRIDGE

I (Maile) was in Hawaii visiting my family over college break. My grandfather, aunt, and I were shopping at the shopping center. As I walked out of the store to take my packages to the car, I heard someone faintly cry out, "Miss, excuse me." At first I didn't realize I was the "Miss." When I did, I just kept walking. I had been taught not to talk to strangers and to be suspicious of others for the sake of safety.

Then I thought, "Wait. What am I doing?" I'm a Bible college student, and have served as a member of Street Team Ministries for three years. I care about those who live on the streets! I say I'm a child of God, but I didn't even turn at the sound of that cry? How are the streets on the East Coast any different than the streets of Honolulu? There was a disconnect in my life. I had always believed that ministry is not just in the pulpit but everywhere you are in daily life. I had lived and ministered this way, but somehow I had compartmentalized what I knew and believed. Besides, this was not a convenient time! I was on vacation, visiting my family and getting things I needed for the coming school year on the mainland.

Questions for Reflection

1. What are some possible factors at the heart of Maile's initial reaction to the woman who called to her? How are they legitimate?

2. In light of the "Reasons for Keeping Our Distance" on p. 118 , assess the college student's conflict in her immediate responses to a needy woman.

3. In what ways do you identify with Maile in this story?

MAILE'S STORY (CONTINUED)

I closed the trunk of my aunt's car. I knew I needed to go back and see if this woman was calling out to me. So many thoughts were running through my mind of why people would advise me not to stop. She would probably just take advantage of me. This was not smart. But in spite of being torn, I knew I had to go back. The woman was sitting off to the side of the little drug store, very broken and sad. Suddenly everything else disappeared, and all I saw was her. I forgot my grandpa and aunt were finishing up in the store and about ready to leave. For me, time was irrelevant now, and I wondered *how could I have passed her by?*

As I got close, I asked the woman if she had been calling me and she said, "Yes." When I asked her if she needed anything, she said she needed money and food. I told her I would get her some food from the store. Then she changed her mind and asked if I could get her cat food instead. The bridge she slept under at night had become her home. Cats came, and they had become her pets and comfort, but they were hungry, too.

As I listened to this woman, I squatted down close to hear her better. She seemed disoriented, and I could smell alcohol. She was dirty, and could barely look me in the eyes. Any dignity was lost and any sense of self-esteem so fragile. I sensed her feelings of worthlessness, as if I were better than her, cleaner than her. Suddenly I realized I had intuitively moved—from standing to squatting to kneeling in front of her to sitting next to her. Wearing my new Christmas clothes, it was as if sitting on the dirty concrete beside this woman was the most natural thing in the world.

Questions for Reflection

1. If you were Maile, would you have gone back to connect with the woman you had tried to ignore? Why or why not? Share a time when that has happened to you.

2. Discuss the correlation between what was happening to Maile mentally, emotionally, and spiritually in this section in relation to what was happening with physical space. Is there a particular point where her "sterile gloves" came off?

3. In getting close to those in great need as Christ did, discuss possible guidelines to give our children, or students like Maile, in an Isaiah 59 world. In doing so, consider whether the boundaries for "safety's

sake" are biblical or Christ-like. How do we decide when to get close and engage and when to refrain?

MAILE'S STORY (CONCLUSION)

I asked the woman under the bridge how she had ended up on the street. Had she tried to tap into any local resources for help? She admitted she had, but that sometimes she was so depressed by the process and the hopelessness she felt. Then she introduced me to her boyfriend and began to tell me more of her story. She had lost everything precious to her. She seemed so honest and genuine. As she spoke we were both crying, and before I knew it, she was in my arms and I held her. It was one of the most beautiful moments I have ever experienced in my life. The woman, whose name I did not know, wiped her tears, looked me in the eyes, and said, "Thank you, thank you so much! *No one has ever done that for me.*"

I was shocked. I hadn't done anything for her yet. She continued, "Don't get me anything. Don't buy me anything. I don't need anything else from you. You just gave me all I needed. *No one has ever done for me what you just did.*" I could barely speak because I didn't know what to say. Finally, all I could say was, "Jesus loves you." Tears were running down her face and mine. I told her I would bring her food because I wanted her to have some. Before leaving I encouraged her to try to get help through the homeless services she had applied for.

I believe I felt God's love with the woman under the bridge in its purest form. All I could see was this woman, her beauty, her pain, her brokenness, and God's love for her. The Scripture says, "He saw, was moved with compassion and he did . . ." Ironically, I had been moved with compassion before and been a part of compassionate ministries, but for the first time I experienced a quality of Jesus' love for a woman I did not know that was personal, unique, and specific. My eyes and heart need to be open to see what *He* sees.

My aunt and grandpa had walked past me and were waiting in the car. They were stunned when they saw me sitting on the ground with this woman. As they waited in the car, they watched what transpired and were amazed as they saw the love of God for the woman under the bridge.

CONCLUDING QUESTIONS FOR REFLECTION

1. What are the most important lessons for you personally from Maile's story?

2. What are the greatest areas of tension for you in the story, and why?

3. To what extent is trust a factor when we come close to someone in need with Christ's compassion? For example, Maile began to believe the woman's story. Discuss whether or not the "truth" of the woman's story is a factor in practicing the compassion of Christ in practical ways.

4. In some cultures, a fear of "being taken advantage of" is considered a legitimate reason for followers of Jesus to refrain from engaging personally with people in great need. Reflect on the extent to which this is a fear of yours and examine it in light of Scripture and Christ's example. Does it, *should it*, make any difference in our response to the need?

CHAPTER 7

THE INTIMATE INJUSTICE
OF SEXUAL EXPLOITATION

Father, the horror of this darkness overwhelms us.
Take fear away, and teach us how to fight.
Awaken ears to silent cries of victims,
Whose eyes speak death, and yet they somehow live.
Fill us with faith that conquers with compassion,
With acts of courage celebrating truth.
Anoint us by your Spirit for the battle,
Free slaves, and turn their horror into hope.
Amen.[38]

Four hundred women were enjoying a joyful time of worship in the women's conference. As women stood to their feet to immerse themselves in song and vibrant praise to God, a number found their way to the front near the worship band and altar to dance freely as they sang. Among those, one woman in particular caught my eye.

She was the most abandoned and demonstrative in her worship. Her red outfit, flashes of gold jewelry, and strong makeup caught my

---

38 Beth Grant and Cindy Hudlin, eds, "Conclusion," in *Hands That Heal: International Curriculum to Train Caregivers of Trafficking Survivors*. (n.p.: Faith Alliance Against Slavery and Trafficking, 2007), 336.

attention and most likely that of others in the conservative church. As I watched this woman dance and twirl with joy, I found myself strangely uncomfortable and struggling not to judge what appeared to me to be ostentatious and even immodest worship. If she wanted attention, my reserved New England sensitivities told me, she was definitely getting that! Another part of me was fighting not to judge, not to notice, and let it be. As the inner battle between human (female!) judgment and grace was waged, my Father's discomforting still small voice broke in: "You are looking at Mary Magdalene."

THE AMERICA WE THOUGHT WE KNEW

Growing up in the 1950s and 1960s in the United States, a majority of Americans saw ourselves as part of a Christian nation. Even if people were not Christian and church-going, a majority of Americans held what were considered Judeo-Christian values. It was not until my college years in the 1970s and that decade's "sexual revolution" that America witnessed a seismic shift in attitudes and practice of sexuality that continues to erode the moral fiber of a nation to this day.

Tragically, over the last ten years, as David and I have traveled America to minister, we have come to the conclusion that our nation was not the nation we thought it was prior to the sexual revolution. Yes, more people went to church during the 1940s to 1960s. But in every church across the nation where we present the story of sexually exploited women and children and the ministry of Project Rescue, we meet women who themselves were victims of child sexual exploitation in America. Women in their fifties and sixties share with brokenness their own pain of abuse as little girls at the hands of fathers, uncles, brothers, grandfathers, or family friends.

Some have found a measure of healing over years in their walk with Jesus and the power of His truth applied to their pain. Others have found the help of excellent Christian counselors whom God has used in their healing process. But sadly, all too many victims have carried their pain of sexual abuse in silence because of shame and intimidation by abusers that no one would believe them.

> There is hope for *all* victims of child sexual exploitation—when they hear the truth about God's love for them and His forgiveness for all sin, and they bring the shame of the past into His healing, loving light.

Abusers of four-year-olds, as incredible as it may seem, tell them it was all their fault, and that "You're a bad girl." And the Enemy of their souls reinforces the secret lies over a lifetime. On many occasions, formerly abused women overflow with tears of gratitude for someone coming to share the story of what God was doing to bring freedom and healing to little girls rescued from brothels in India. For many, it was the first time they had heard this evil, intimate injustice shared in the church in the context of hope. "And if there is hope for little girls born in brothels, surely there is hope for me!"

Yes, thank you, Jesus, there is hope for *all* victims of child sexual exploitation—when they hear the truth about God's love for them and His forgiveness for all sin, and they bring the shame of the past into His healing, loving light. But sickeningly, "Christian America" had far too many male family members—many who went to church on Sundays—practicing secret sexual sin with little girls. *It was not the America we thought it was.*

THE GLOBAL INTIMATE INJUSTICE
OF SEXUAL EXPLOITATION

Along with the rest of the world's nations, Americans (yes, Christians in America) must face the evil of sexual abuse and exploitation in their own cities, towns, and homes. Incest, child abuse, rape, domestic sexual violence, pornography, prostitution, and sex trafficking in all its insidious forms has and is occurring with alarming frequency.

> Human compassion is selective, and unfortunately this is even true of Christians. But Christ's compassion is not.

First, we as followers of Jesus must acknowledge the uncomfortable truth that it is happening—and sometimes, it is happening where we would least expect it. This is essential if we are to address the injustice and help both victims and perpetrators find the deliverance, healing, and transformation that Christ promised to all who would call upon His name for help. Human compassion is selective, and unfortunately this is even true of Christians. But Christ's compassion is not. That's foundational to the good news of God's grace and the gospel. God sent His Son to seek and save the lost and promises new life to all who call upon His name and begin the journey of faith: both for the child or woman abused and for their male and female abusers who need to acknowledge their sins and find deliverance as well. Christ's compassion in life-changing dynamic with His truth and Spirit is radically given to all who will receive! It's through God's redemptive missional lens that we take a look at the scope of the most intimate form of injustice in our world.[39]

A GLIMPSE INTO THE EXTENT OF CHILD SEXUAL EXPLOITATION (CSE) GLOBALLY

A summary of some of the statistics related to sexual injustice in its diverse forms is helpful to understand the scope of the most intimate forms of injustice.

- An estimated 2 million children a year are victimized globally for child sexual exploitation (CSE). [40] This does not include those exploited for non-commercial purposes.

- International studies reveal that approximately 20 percent of women and 5 to 10 percent of men report being victims of sexual violence as children.[41]

- Studies suggest that a significant minority of children in Europe, between 10 and 20 percent, are sexually assaulted during their childhood.[42]

---

39 Many readers may already be aware of and involved in the needs of the sexually exploited through their professional work as social workers, lawyers, law enforcement, medical professionals, public educators or trauma counselors. All play necessary, critical roles in the battle against sexual exploitation and trafficking. In contrast, the purpose of this chapter is to provide a window into the world of sexual exploitation for people of faith who are often sheltered from it. The goal is to provide information on the topic in the context of a biblical understanding of Christ's mission and the great compassionate mission given to His followers that flows from it.

40 Office to Combat and Monitor Trafficking in Persons, U.S. State Department, "Trafficking in Persons Report 13," June 2010.

41 World Health Organization, "Fact Sheets: Violence against Women," http://www.who.int/mediacentre/factsheets/fs239/en.

42 European Commission Home Affairs, "Child Sexual Abuse," http://ec.europa.eu/dgs/home-affairs/what-we-do/policies/organized-crime-and-human-trafficking/child-sexual-abuse/index_en.htm.

- The International Labour Organisation (ILO)
  estimates that of the child victims of forced labor
  worldwide, as many as one million are also victims of
  sexual exploitation.[43]

- According to the Optional Protocol to the
  Convention on the Rights of the Child on the
  sale of children,[44] child prostitution, and child
  pornography, the prostitution of children globally
  is often orchestrated by networks of pimps and
  organized crime to generate income. Children are
  also prostituted by family members and community
  members in exchange for food, drugs, clothing,
  housing, and other goods.

- ECPAT International estimates that over 20 percent
  of sex trafficking victims worldwide are children.[45]

- In the nation of Brazil alone, it is estimated there
  are over 500,000 prostituted children.[46] When global
  sports events convene (for example, the World Cup),
  the number of sexually exploited children explodes
  to accommodate the destructive desires of men who
  will pay for sex with a child.

---

43 ECPAT, "FAQs," http://www.ecpat.net/faqs.

44 United Nations Human Rights: Office of the High Commissioner for Human Rights,
    "Optional Protocol to the Convention on the Rights of the Child," http://www.ohchr.
    org/EN/ProfessionalInterest/Pages/OPSCCRC.aspx.

45 United Nations Human Rights: Office of the High Commissioner for Human Rights,
    "Optional Protocol to the Convention on the Rights of the Child," http://www.ohchr.
    org/EN/ProfessionalInterest/Pages/OPSCCRC.aspx.

46 ECPAT, "FAQs," http://www.ecpat.net/faqs.

- Child sex abuse is an everyday reality for as many as half of India's children.[47] Home to more than 375 million children (roughly equivalent to the total population of the United States!) comprising nearly 40 percent of the country's population, India has the largest number of minors of any country in the world, and the world's largest number of sexually abused children.

The Internet has only compounded the horrific effect of child sex abuse on victims and the amount of pornographic content available to those addicted globally to this destructive appetite. Online file-sharing networks, listservs, and over 1,500 websites dedicated solely to child pornography disseminate exploitive and explicit images of victims freely and instantly around the globe. The European Commission Home Affairs website explains:

Every day, countless children around the world are sexually abused and exploited, and images and videos of the abuse are circulated. Already in 2005, an estimated one million child sexual abuse images were online. Fifty thousand new child abuse images are added each year. More than 70 percent of reported images feature children below ten years of age. And these images never disappear. Children that have been identified and rescued years ago still have to face the fact that their abuse remains freely

47 "Hidden Darkness: Child Sexual Abuse in India," Asia Sentinel, May 2007, http://www.asiasentinel.com/society/hidden-darkness-child-sexual-abuse-in-india. Reference from a thirteen-state National Study on Child Sexual Abuse conducted by the Ministry of Women and Child Development, UNICEF, and Save The Children.

available for anyone to view online, and are revictimized over and over.[48]

Pornography is no "victimless" crime!

A GLIMPSE INTO THE EXTENT OF CHILD SEXUAL EXPLOITATION IN THE UNITED STATES

As in the case of child sex exploitation (CSE) globally, in the United States solid statistics are difficult to come by since child victims tend not to report due to fear, intimidation, and/or shame. Here are some of the best estimates growing out of research in the US, which are generally assumed to be conservative due to under-reporting of these kinds of crimes.

- One in five girls and one in twenty boys is a victim of child sexual abuse (CSA).[49] CSA includes a range of sexual behaviors between an adult and child, including sexual bodily contact, forcing children to watch pornography, exploiting children as prostitutes, or forcing them to perform in pornography.[50] Since child sex abuse occurs for the sexual gratification of

---

48 European Commission Home Affairs, "A Global Alliance against Child Sexual Abuse Online," http://ec.europa.eu/dgs/home-affairs/what-we-do/policies/orga-nized-crime-and-human-trafficking/global-alliance-against-child-abuse/index_en.htm.

49 David Finkelhor, Director of the Crimes Against Children Research Center quoted in "Child Sex Abuse Statistics," http://www.victimsofcrime.org/media/report-ing-on-child-sexual-abuse/child-sexual-abuse-statistics.

50 United States Department of Veterans Affairs, "Child Sexual Abuse," http://www.ptsd.va.gov/public/pages/child-sexual-abuse.asp.

the offending adult, little concern is given for the long-term traumatic effect on the child.

- Over the course of their lifetime, 28 percent of US youth ages fourteen to seventeen surveyed had been sexually victimized.[51]

- Children are most vulnerable to CSA between the ages of seven and thirteen.[52]

- About three out of ten of those who sexually abuse children are family members of the child. This includes fathers, grandfathers, or brothers.[53] However, it can also include others the child knows, like a neighbor, teacher, or family friend.

- According to the National Child Abuse and Neglect Data System (NCANDS), an estimated 9.3 percent of confirmed or substantiated child abuse and neglect cases in 2005 involved sexual abuse (US Department of Health and Human Services, 2007). This figure translates into over 83,800 victims in 2005 alone (USDHHS, 2007).[54]

- An estimated 300,000 children and adolescents are the victims of domestic trafficking and commercial sexual exploitation in the US *every year*.[55]

---

51 Finkelhor.

52 Ibid.

53 United States Department of Veterans Affairs, "Child Sexual Abuse."

54 American Humane Association, "Child Sexual Abuse," http://www.americanhumane. org/children/stop-child-abuse/fact-sheets/child-sexual-abuse.html.

55 UNICEF, "Child Sexual Exploitation in the USA: Not Just a Problem for Developing Nations," http://www.unicef.org/infobycountry/usa_46464.html.

A GLIMPSE INTO THE EXTENT OF SEXUAL VIOLENCE AGAINST WOMEN GLOBALLY

According to the Sexual Violence Research Initiative, sexual violence is defined as any sexual act, attempt to obtain a sexual act, unwanted sexual comments or advances, or acts to traffic, or otherwise directed, against a person's sexuality using coercion, by any person regardless of their relationship to the victim, in any setting, including but not limited to home and work. It includes rape by strangers, systematic rape during armed conflict, sexual harassment, sexual abuse of children, sexual abuse of people with mental and physical disabilities, forced prostitution and sexual trafficking, child marriage, denial of the right to use contraception, forced abortion, and violent acts against the sexual integrity of women, including female genital cutting and obligatory inspections for virginity.[56]

- An estimated 35 percent of women worldwide have experienced either intimate partner violence or nonpartner sexual violence in their lifetime.[57]

- Globally, women and girls represent 98 percent of the estimated 4.5 million persons forced into sexual exploitation.[58]

- During times of armed conflict or natural disasters with their accompanying breakdown of social, political, and family infrastructure, women and children are

---

56 Sexual Violence Research Initiative, "FAQ," http://www.svri.org/faq.htm

57 World Health Organization, Fact Sheets, "Violence against Women," http://www.who.int /mediacentre/factsheets/fs239/en.

58 UN WOMEN, "Facts and Figures: Ending Violence against Women," http://www.unwomen.org./en/what-we-do/ending-violence-against-women/facts-and-figures.

especially vulnerable to acts of sexual violence. All too common, violence includes rape by combatants, and ironically by humanitarian aid workers.[59]

LET'S JUST GET PAST THE FACTS?

Perhaps by now, some readers skipped reading many or all of the disturbing facts about sexual injustice above and just decided to continue reading here. For some, they are uncomfortable, unimaginable, unwelcome details we'd rather not read. It's too much information about sexual violence you cannot imagine or really believe is so prevalent. Perhaps you think the author is making too much of this. You have a feeling a lot of those girls or women privately wanted it—so perhaps it's not actually exploitation? For other women readers, you stopped because the details of intimate injustice are too painful, because it's your very own private— possibly secret—story. For some male readers, you avoided reading details because you have participated in sexual exploitation yourself somewhere in your journey—perhaps before you began to follow Jesus, or sadly since—either face-to-face or through pornography. And perhaps you still blame her for tempting you, because she was promiscuous? *But read on.*

There is hope in Christ for all of us who read: those hurting from wounds in the past, those who have wounded and live in shame, and those who sense God's heart and want to understand and help in the healing process. His love, hope, and forgiveness are for *all* of us! So what do all these hard statistics about sexual exploitation from

---

59 World Health Organization Fact Sheets, "Sexual and Reproductive Health: Sexual Violence," http://www.who.int/reproductivehealth/topics/violence/sexual_violence/en/index.html.

secular organizations and agencies have to do with good people of faith who want to practice courageous compassion?

> *If we don't know, we can't understand.*
> *If we don't understand, we tend to judge.*
> *And when we judge, we cause more hurt, more shame, more pain.*
> *And the lies of the enemy of each person's soul continue to destroy unquestioned.*
> *Because good people, God's people, don't discern the truth from the lies and fight for those broken and bound for whom the Jesus we say we love died.*

THE REST OF THE STORY

The Father who loves chastened and opened my heart while I was judging the woman in red as she worshipped her Father who loves. There is always a story.

The woman who worshipped God with such passion had been abandoned by her mother as a baby. So began the life of a little girl, then a young girl, then a teenage girl—going from foster home to foster home. Some foster parents are loving, kind, and life-giving. But that was not this child's story. Tragically, she experienced sexual abuse from the time she can remember at the hands of those who should have been her protectors. The rejection that began with her mother continued and became painfully layered with the physical, emotional, psychological, and spiritual trauma of sexual exploitation. The natural, innate God-given boundaries of what is healthy, loving, and appropriate were never modeled for her to see in a family that loved her.

Additionally, a God-ordained sense of identity and healthy female sexuality was violated and marred before there was even a chance for it to mature. In her formative years, her very identity and perceived value as a girl became defined by inappropriate sexual relationships. Even though she was the victim, she became in her own eyes and the eyes of the world "the girl who is bad." Her innocence, her dignity, her value, and her purity were all violently wrenched from her, but the blame would be hers to carry.

Then, like Mary Magdalene, somewhere on the journey of exploitation, rejection, shame, and an identity marred by sexual sin, she miraculously met Jesus. She learned He does love, He does forgive, He does save, He does redeem from sin. And He gives her hope for a redeemed future with dignity as His daughter. Thankfully, God's grace meets us where we are and moves us redemptively, lovingly from there as we seek Him with all of our hearts.

If Jesus' relationship with Mary Magdalene is shared in Scripture (Luke 7:36–50) for our insight and admonition, and for the sake of the men who watched, then perhaps the jubilant worship and demeanor of the woman in red is more our problem than hers. When Mary Magdalene walked into a room full of men straight to the One she was learning to love, no one was comfortable—except Jesus. When she broke the expensive perfume over her soon-to-be Savior's feet, it was totally inappropriate—except to Jesus. When she caressed His feet with her hair, it was undeniably sensual in any culture—except to Jesus. The only One who was genuinely without sin defended Mary's culturally inappropriate, but inwardly beautiful, devotion and rebuked the self-righteous men who watched her in judgment. (In all fairness, there were probably several women in the household cooking and serving who also would have been aghast and had their own scorn for this woman.) But Jesus publicly forgave

Mary's sins and proclaimed to her and all who would hear, "Your faith has saved you. Go in peace"(Luke 7:50). He further proclaimed that wherever the gospel was preached in the world, Mary's act of worship would be remembered (Matt. 26:13). And so it is!

THE MYSTERIOUS LINK BETWEEN A WOMAN'S SEXUAL EXPERIENCES AND HER IDENTITY

When the ministry of Project Rescue began in 1997 with prostituted women and children in the red-light districts in India, David and I knew little of the world of prostitution. It is traditionally not a world that followers of Jesus visit, and while often only blocks away from our churches, it is worlds away from the one we know. So we wanted to learn all we could as quickly as possible in order to understand how best to minister to women and children who had been prostituted. In listening to victims' stories, caregivers' insights, observing their healing journeys, and doing much research over these years, one of the effects of prostitution and sexual abuse that has been most disturbing and complex to understand is the effect of the most intimate forms of injustice on the victim's literal identity. Especially for women and girls who have been sexually violated, over time what has happened to them sexually becomes how they view their whole identity . . . no more, no less. Tragically, this is also how society, and possibly even the church, tends to define women and girls who have been sexually exploited or caught in sexual sin. "She's the one who was sexually abused as a child." "She's the woman who had an affair with the pastor." "She's a slut." "She was a prostitute." Period.

In the case of prostituted women and children, the systematic, intentional, and violent deconstruction of any prior identity in the victim except "prostitute" and "whore" is cruelly accomplished by pimps and madams to create and control a "new" woman or child who is intimidated through violence, profitable for sex, controllable, and bound by her or his new identity. In Melissa Farley's respected work, *Prostitution, Trafficking, and Traumatic Stress*,[60] she explains that the acts perpetrated on women in prostitution leave behind not only a physical impact; they also psychologically define her as an object. The prostituted woman or child is reduced to her body parts and is forced to act the part of whatever men want her to be. Farley describes this destructive process:

> Despite the clarity of many analysts on this topic, there is a lack of knowledge among clinicians regarding the systematic methods of brainwashing, indoctrination (called "seasoning" by pimps), and physical control that are used against women in prostitution. *These techniques are specifically aimed at eliminating any corner of mental space for her to exist in* [emphasis mine]. The strategies of political torturers: debilitation, dread, and dependency, read like a pimp's manual. The unpredictable and extreme violence in prostitution, *like that in torture, is not only used for economic and sadistic reasons.* It ultimately physically impresses upon the woman that she is utterly worthless and that she is socially nonexistent except as a prostitute.

This deliberate eradication of a young girl's or woman's identity as created by God with dignity for good purposes, and the forced creation of a new identity as a sex object, is facilitated

---

60 Melissa Farley, ed., *Prostitution, Trafficking, and Traumatic Stress* (Binghamton, NY: Haworth Maltreatment and Trauma Press, 2003), xiv–xv.

by giving the girl a new name for the "business," different clothes, and makeup—all to define this new female persona whose only value is for purchased sex. Her introduction into this new life of exploitation, and the obliteration of all that came before, is usually ushered in with violent rape or gang rapes over a period of weeks, months, even years.

Former Coexecutive Director of the Coalition Against Trafficking in Women in New York, Dorchen Leidholdt, sheds more light on this same destructive initiating process used by exploiters in the sex industry, and on its long-term impact on the victim:[61]

> The sex industry entrepreneur "turns out" a woman or girl by eradicating her identity, erasing her sense of self, especially any belief that she is entitled to dignity and bodily integrity. "Turning out" often takes place through rape and acts of sexual humiliation. It is facilitated by changing her name, giving her a "makeover" to ensure that she will be viewed as a sex object, alienating her from her family and friends, instilling in her the belief that she is an "outlaw," rejected by yet superior to "straight" society, and teaching her to accept her place in a rigid hierarchy, where she is obedient to the man who profits from the sale of her body and any woman he designates as his surrogate.

The prostituted woman or child has entered a world of brutal control and hierarchy in which any question or challenge on her part results in violence, intimidation, and even more rape.

---

61 Dorchen A. Leidholt, "Prostitution and Trafficking in Women: An Intimate Relationship," in Farley, 172–173.

It's only the beginning of a lifetime of sexual violence and degradation in which, over time, many prostituted women and children begin to fragment psychologically and experience dissociative disorders (formerly termed "multiple personality disorder").[62] What is happening to them day after day is so emotionally, mentally, physically, and spiritually traumatic that the dissociative state becomes a shield to handle the unthinkable, unbearable, intolerable. And the woman or child who existed before will never exist as she was again.

> God's grace expressed through Christ is *unmerited favor*. Selective— natural human— compassion is an inaccurate reflection of Christ's heart and mission.

A COMPASSION CHECK

"But how do we know if they were really trafficked or forced to have sex with men—or if they really chose it?" Those of us who minister to women and children in sexual slavery often hear this question spoken or implied from many good people who care about trafficking and its victims. Over time and meeting and ministering to many victims of sexual exploitation in a number of countries, my own question has become, "Does it matter how they got there? If it does, why? Does it change our willingness to minister the love and compassion of Christ for those in slavery?"

---

62 Ibid., 173.

If it matters to us how a woman or child ended up on the street being prostituted, if that is a determination for our compassion as followers of Jesus (as it is to law enforcement and legal aid), then we probably struggle reading this chapter. If we prioritize assigning blame and knowing who is "the victim" (trafficked) vs. the "immoral woman"(prostitute) in order to determine our "appropriate" level of compassion, we are missing the nature of Christ's compassion altogether. God's grace expressed through Christ is *unmerited favor.* Selective—natural human—compassion is an inaccurate reflection of Christ's heart and mission. It is an especially misleading dichotomy when ministering to women and children in sexual slavery for the following reasons.

1. Unless one has a long-term relationship with an exploited woman or child and has earned their trust, they will probably not share the intimate details of their story of exploitation. If they feel pressured to do so, it will most likely be a sanitized, safe version. If there has been severe psychological trauma, caregivers may never know the true, full story. Should that keep us from ministering Christ's love, healing and hope?

2. Many women being prostituted on the street are afraid to share how they got there. They may act as if they want to be there, portraying some semblance of autonomy that, in actuality, does not exist. It's a protective mechanism to deny their lack of control over their own bodies and lives.

3. Madams and female brothel owners have a complex story. If they have been raped, exploited as young girls, and/or trafficked into prostitution, the only way to escape the daily exploitation is often to become part of the economic system by exploiting other younger women. Often, today's exploiters were yesterday's victims in a different context. So assigning blame and our compassionate response is really complicated if those categories are our condition for being compassionate.

4. No adult in the world of sexual injustice is totally pure and blameless. As Romans 3:23 states, "All have sinned and fall short of the glory of God." No adult in the world of sexual injustice is totally outside the possibility of God's redemptive mission, however; John 1:12 reminds us that "To all who did receive him, to those who believed in his name, he gave the right to become children of God." Christ's compassion and mission are radical in scope and beyond our limited human compassion and sense of justice.

Yes, we face constant inner tension as followers of Jesus in learning to live out His compassion to sex offenders, madams, corrupt policeman, and pimps, as well as their victims. It is not a black and white world, and our compassion at times is mixed with anger and indignation. Heidi, a young college student in summer ministry in Asia, shares this struggle in her journal with raw honesty.[63]

---

63 Heidi's blog, "Not for the Cause, but for the People", June 12, 2013.

The last brothel we visited was run by a madam that we were specifically visiting. Her granddaughter is in our ministry's aftercare home. She [the madam] had come to the home and given her granddaughter to them stating, "I don't want her to turn out like me." We sat down on her bed and she shook our hands, thanking us so much for taking care of her granddaughter. She was so excited to hear that my friend and I had come all the way (to her country) just to help out with the girls. We explained that we were just beginning to teach her granddaughter English, and she was catching on quickly. The grandmother's eyes filled with tears.

Then I looked out of her window, which overlooked the rows of soiled curtains. I saw one "worker" slapped in the face by a customer, and she began to weep. Utter devastation was occurring right outside her bedroom window, and she was the business owner. I remember thinking, "Lord, did your grace run out?"

The madam offered all of us a bottle of Sprite. I took it and put it right back on the dresser. In this country, it is considered very rude to not receive what the host gives you as their guest . . . and I knew it. Like I was going to receive her hospitality and drink anything from her? I'd rather throw it up against the wall than drink it! My host looked at me with saddened eyes and nodded her head as if to say she understood. She looked at us very intentionally and said, "Thank you."

But God had decided to answer my angry question. "No, My grace has not run out—but yours did. Drink it."

I lifted the bottle up to my lips and felt the stinging "grace" go down my throat. I drank most of it. The madam was honored that I had received her hospitality. That's what giving grace to others who don't deserve it can be like sometimes. It may sting at first, but then it refreshes your soul. . . . There are not only girls involved in this process (of sexual slavery), but madams and sick customers that come through every day. Show them grace, especially when they're trying to do something "right" and get their granddaughter out of the hell they've created. Drink their Sprite. It'll sting, but just shut up, and drink it.

THE CRITICAL ROLE OF THE CHURCH FOR THE SEXUALLY EXPLOITED AND ENSLAVED

The summary of estimated numbers of women and children who have endured some form of sexual violence and exploitation in our world is staggering, as are the victims' resulting physical, mental, emotional, and spiritual needs. Sadly, from culture to culture, human beings tend to stigmatize women, men and children on the basis of what has happened to them sexually. They buy into the lie of Satan that a woman or child who has been prostituted, raped, abused, or behaved promiscuously is "damaged goods" and has little to no value, identity, or future beyond their negative sexual experience(s). Part of the twisted cruelty of the lie is that even if they were children at the time, it is said to be their own fault!

So who—besides courageously compassionate followers of Jesus—can possibly see twenty-first century Tamars, Rahabs, Mary Magdalenes, and women caught in adultery through the

> In a dark world with an increasingly distorted view of sexuality, the church has a critical role to play, a life-changing message to share with victims of sexual exploitation.

compassionate eyes of Jesus? If not followers of Jesus individually or the community of faith, who has the faith and courage to believe—or cares enough to believe—that millions of victims of sexual violence and sin are still men and women given life by a loving God and can be redeemed for a new life with good, God-ordained purposes? Yes, in a dark world with an increasingly distorted view of sexuality, the church has a critical role to play, a life-changing message to share with victims of sexual exploitation in all its sordid, despicable, destructive forms. But we must search our souls and ask ourselves some tough questions.

1. Can we, God's children, become voices of a message of hope for all men, women, boys, and girls—regardless of their sexual history—based on the life-giving person and message of Jesus Christ? In Christ's own words, He came "to seek and to save the lost" (Luke 19:10).

2. Will we, God's children, accept our responsibility as proclaimers of His promise that all who believe in Christ receive a new redeemed identity in Him? No one needs that promise and friendship on the redemptive journey more than those who have

had their God-given identities and value trampled
through sexual violence.

3. Will we, God's children who know His liberating
   truth, seize the opportunity and share that truth with
   those who are in sexual bondage (John 8:31–32)?
   The sexually exploited have lived with lies spoken to
   them, over them, and about them, and too often this
   has taken place from childhood. The opportunity
   for liberation can only be fulfilled by those who
   personally know and walk in God's liberating
   truth themselves.

4. Will we, God's children who know that He sent
   Jesus to heal our bodies and minds as well as
   save our souls, share that promise personally and
   compassionately with the sexually exploited
   (Isa. 53:4–6)? Yes, as with all of us who have come to
   Christ, sometimes healing is a moment, sometimes
   it's a journey over years. But some of the mental and
   emotional scars of the sexually exploited can only
   be healed by the One who literally died because He
   loved them. If the church does not take this message
   to the millions who are being and have been sexually
   violated, how will they know that healing, salvation,
   and a new identity in Christ with God-given dignity
   is possible?

If a pastor, church leaders, and members are committed to
reaching their city or town with the life-changing message of the
gospel, they cannot ignore the sexually wounded and still hope to

achieve this goal. If we have a vision to change our nation, we cannot ignore the sexually exploited among us and still do so. If we have a missional heart to impact the nations, we cannot ignore the millions of "walking dead" whose spirits have died through sexual violence and still somehow believe we are impacting the nations. May we be the church where men, women, and children in sexual slavery are welcome to walk in just as they are, and experience the life-changing love of Jesus and begin their spiritual journeys through the liberating power of the Holy Spirit. May we as followers of Jesus become known as people of compassion and faith for those who have been victims of the most intimate forms of brutal injustice.

If we become a people who practice this kind of courageous compassion to the sexually exploited, we will not have room in our churches for all who will come to find hope, freedom, healing, and the Jesus who loves them. Our churches will be the supportive communities of grace that are so essential for victims of injustice in the messy but redemptive process of transformation.

A CALL FOR THE CHURCH TO ENGAGE IN PREVENTION OF SEXUAL EXPLOITATION

Several years ago, my husband and I participated in a regional anti-trafficking conference in Kansas City, Missouri. One of the most chilling moments of our lives was listening to an interview with an incarcerated pimp conducted in Dallas, Texas. With arrogance, this man described how he and other pimps could walk into any mall in America, and within minutes, walk out with a young teenage girl who would disappear with him into the world of prostitution.

When the law enforcement interviewer questioned his claim and how he could possibly do that so quickly with an unsuspecting teenager, he bragged about having radar for unhappy young girls who didn't feel good about themselves. He and pimps like him zero in on those who apparently have low self-esteem and are alone, and begin a conversation. It went something like this:

> *Pimp: "Hey, are you OK?"*
> *Young girl: "Why?"*
> *Pimp: "You look like something's botherin' you."*
> *Young girl: "Yeah, I guess it is."*
> *Pimp: "Your family?"*
> *Young girl: "Yeah."*
> *Pimp: "They don't understand you, do they?"*
> *Young girl: "How do you know . . . ?"*
> *Pimp: "Hey, girl, you're beautiful. Do they tell you that?"*
> *Young girl begins to share her unhappiness and conflict at home . . .*
> *Pimp: "Girl, you're beautiful. They don't understand you! You come with me and I'll give you everything you want— beautiful clothes, jewelry. I'll take you places—you can stay with me. "*

Within minutes of the meeting, an unhappy young girl already contemplating running away leaves a mall with a man she doesn't know, because anything seems better than what is happening at home, or in foster care, or when alone with her mother's boyfriend. The pimp summarized the key to his power over vulnerable young teenage girls: "I tell them everything they're dying to hear at home that their parents are not telling them." And they disappear at the rate of up to 300,000 a year, in the United States, into the world of trafficking and prostitution.

One of the most needed ministries of the church that can make young children and teenagers less vulnerable to sexual exploitation and trafficking in our sexually violent world is mentoring them into a healthy identity as a young son or daughter of God. Those teenagers who are followers of Jesus and who have a strong sense of their value and dignity in Him are less vulnerable than those whose sense of worth is distorted by the way their marred, hyper-sexualized culture defines their value. Tragically, as American and Western European cultures increasingly sell inappropriate sexuality in all its forms as normative, our children by default internalize this American/Western cultural view of themselves and their sexuality—unless Christian parents, leaders, and the church provide them with a healthy, positive, biblical view of sexuality. When our children from elementary school on up are inundated with non-Christian views presented as "facts," we as followers of Jesus and the church can no longer afford to remain silent about sexuality.

> When our children from elementary school on up are inundated with non-Christian views presented as "facts," we as followers of Jesus and the church can no longer afford to remain silent about sexuality.

One woman who understands the importance of nurturing a strong sense of identity in Christ and value as a daughter of God into young girls and teenagers is Mary Mahon of Latin American Child Care. Several years ago, when she recognized the growing tide of sexual violence against young girls in Costa Rica where she worked, Mary prayerfully determined to do something preventive while girls were still in upper elementary school to help them become less vulnerable to exploitation. Chicas de Promesa (Girls of Promise) clubs[64] were the realization of that dream and of Mary's commitment with her partners to stand up against this evil.

Chicas de Promesa is a girls' empowerment club. In Mary's words, "It is a safe place where girls can study and be mentored, build friendships and have fun. It helps girls at risk realize their dignity, no matter what they have been through; it strengthens them to overcome their current challenges, and prepares them for the future they dream of: all within an atmosphere of God's love and promises." Most of the girls are sadly familiar with sexual exploitation in their daily lives, as mothers sell their bodies to feed their families. Fortunately, girls who attend Chicas de Promesa are also students at the partnering Latin America Child Care schools, where the same values are instilled in vulnerable girls through Christian education. This girls' empowerment program, which mentors young girls to realize their God-given value and identity in Christ, is an inspiring example of Christ-centered community programs in partnership with local communities of faith being proactive to protect the vulnerable in contexts of rampant sexual exploitation.

The following topics need to be considered prayerfully from a biblical perspective and become a part of our personal and church discipleship for our children in age-appropriate ways in order to strengthen them against exploitation while helping them live healthier whole lives as God intended.

- How does God, the creator of sexuality, view sexuality? How can we celebrate this gift of God in healthy ways in different stages of our lives?

---

64 See Chicas de Promesa, Latin America Child Care, lacc4hope.org.

- What is the value of the girl child? Why does she have value in God's eyes? (This is critical for girls and for boys to understand, especially when our culture is defining her value as a teenager by how many guys want to sleep with her!)

- What is the value of sexual purity and why? How does it affect our lives for good?

- What is pornography and why is it literally addictive? How is it destructive in effect to all involved? How can a boy, girl, man, woman find help and freedom if they are already addicted?

- What is the affect/cost emotionally, physically, mentally, and spiritually of sexual impurity, promiscuity, and immorality? What is God's view, and how does He see and love those who are sexually impure, promiscuous, or immoral? What is His provision for those who fail?

- How should we as followers of Jesus view ourselves sexually, and how can we live in purity as His followers—as children, teenagers, young adults, adults, and senior adults?

- How can we recognize sexual predators who say they "love" us? How can we recognize traffickers and make ourselves less vulnerable?

- Why is purity so important for marriage, and how can we celebrate and enjoy sexuality in marriage?

- How does God view and relate to men and women who practice homosexual lifestyles? How does

He view homosexuality? What is the difference
between those two questions and responses and their
implications for us as God's children?

Some readers may be asking
by now why in the world we would
be addressing all these topics in
our church's Christian education
and discipleship initiatives—
especially for children? Our
silence is damning. If we are not
intentionally discussing these
sex-related questions in the
community of faith from God's
perspective, our young children,
teenagers, families, and future
ministers are being verbally and
nonverbally coached daily into secular, promiscuous, immoral,
destructive, cultural, unbiblical views and values of sexuality. And
we wonder why our children mirror their culture, the media, and
their peers who talk about, view, and act out these topics nonstop?
It's time godly parents, God's people, and God's church offer
our children and young people an aware, informed, healthy, and
biblical perspective of sexuality. It may well change the course of
their lives, and possibly, their eternities.

> It's time godly parents, God's people, and God's church offer our children and young people an aware, informed, healthy, and biblical perspective of sexuality.

CONCLUSION

The writer of the gospel of John shares an illuminating story of
Jesus and how He related to those who have fallen into sexual

sin. In John 7, he tells the story of an unnamed woman brought before Jesus by religious leaders because she had been caught having sex with a man who was not her husband. One wonders, *was he not caught as well?* No, the religious leaders only brought the adulterous woman to Jesus for judgment and death. Their spoken agenda was concern for fulfilling the law; their hidden agenda was to further their political purposes against Jesus. This woman caught in sin was their pawn.

> For every victim and perpetrator of the most intimate forms of injustice in our world, there is hope, forgiveness, and a future of freedom to be found in Jesus, our Redeemer, Healer, and Lord.

Jesus' response reverberates down through humanity's sordid history of marred sexual injustice and sin. First, He said nothing. Silence. He did not rehearse the Ten Commandments, which He himself had authored as part of the Godhead. He did not shame her. He did not renounce her.

When Jesus finally broke the silence with the shamed woman at His feet, He looked at the waiting religious leaders and said, "Let any one of you who is without sin be the first to throw a stone at her" (John 8:7).

There was One there in that pivotal moment—a defining moment for all sinners then and all sinners who would come—who could have thrown the first stone on the basis of the Law, because He alone was without sin. If Jesus had thrown the first stone, it would have been the first of many thrown by her accusers—themselves full of sin—as they crushed the condemned woman to death. And mankind's hypocritical tendency to overlook our own sin while we self-righteously condemn the sins of others (especially sexual sins!) would have been reinforced.

But the Christ who came intentionally, purposefully to earth for sinners of every kind drew an inerasable line of grace and forgiveness in the sand that day that reverberates for over two thousand years across time and place. "Neither do I condemn you. Go, and sin no more."

For every victim and perpetrator of the most intimate forms of injustice in our world, there is hope, forgiveness, and a future of freedom to be found in Jesus, our Redeemer, Healer, and Lord.

SUGGESTED LEARNING EXPERIENCE

Given the sensitive nature of sexual injustice and its pain, pray together in your small group for victims of sexual exploitation as a needy population whom Christ loves and whom He died for. Pray for those in your community, pray for those in your church. After prayer, consider the following together:

1. What thoughts, feelings, or memories did the chapter produce in you? Why?

2. Are you a person of compassion for victims of sexual exploitation, prostitution, and those who exploit? How different is the emotion that each of those categories of people elicit in you?

3. How can we be more transformed in Christ's image in relating and loving and supporting victims?

4. Like the author, remember a time when you saw someone worship differently and you were uncomfortable. Share and discuss that experience through the lens of this chapter. Pray together for forgiveness for the times when you may have judged inappropriately and for God's wisdom in helping the broken rather than adding to their identity distorted by Satan's condemning lies.

5. Are topics related to biblical sexuality a part of your child and youth education/ministry programs at church? Consider how existing programs could be strengthened to protect and prevent children and youth from vulnerability.

6. Pray about and propose possible next steps.

FOR FURTHER STUDY

- Buff, Esther. "Counseling Sexually Exploited Children." *In Healing for Hurting Hearts: A Handbook for Counseling Children and Youth in Crisis*, edited by Phyllis Kilbourn. Ft. Washington, PA: CLC Publications, 2013.

- ECPAT USA. "Sex Trafficking of Children in the United States: Overview and Issues for Congress. http://ecpatusa.org/wp/wp-content/uploads/2013/08/CRS-Report-R41878_sex-trafficking-of-children.pdf.

- Grant, Beth, and Cindy Hudlin, eds. *Hands That Heal: International Curriculum to Train Caregivers of Trafficking Survivors* (Academic Edition). N.p.: Faith Alliance Against Slavery and Trafficking (FAAST), 2007.

- Human Rights Watch. "India: Child Sex Abuse Shielded by Silence and Neglect." February 2013. http://www.hrw.org/news/2013/02/07/india-child-sex-abuse-shielded-silence-and-neglect.

- Kilbourn, Phyllis. *Sexually Exploited Children: Working to Protect and Heal*. Monrovia, CA: MARC Publications, 1998.

- Leidholt, Dorchen A. "Prostitution and Trafficking in Women: An Intimate Relationship." In

Prostitution, Trafficking, and Traumatic Stress, edited by Melissa Farley. Binghampton, NY: The Haworth Press, 2003.

- Minnesota Indian Women's Resource Center. "Shattered Hearts: The Commercial Sexual Exploitation of American Indian Women and Girls." Summary Report, November 2009.

- Smith, Linda, with Cindy Coloma. *Renting Lacy: A Story of America's Prostituted Children.* Vancouver, WA: Shared Hope International, 2011.

- United States Department of Education: Office of Elementary and Secondary Education. "Human Trafficking of Children in the United States: A Fact Sheet for Schools." http://www2.ed.gov/about/offices/list/oese/oshs/factsheet.html.

- United States Department of State. U.S. State Department Trafficking in Persons Report, 2013. http://www.state.gov/j/tip/rls/tiprpt/2013

CHAPTER 8

COMMUNITY OF DARKNESS, COMMUNITY OF LIGHT: THE CATALYST OF COMMUNITY

The church/community is not incidental to God's purposes
but at the heart of it. Proclamation is not simply an individual
task but a community task, transforming community.[65]

From the darkness outside, she wandered into the back door of
the red-light district church, dutifully following her mother.
Petite, beautiful, and terribly thin, this little daughter couldn't have
been more than four years old. As her mother slipped into the back
pew with a man following, the little girl stood patiently by the end
of the pew. She was dressed in colorful clothes, little sandals, and
charcoaled dark eyes. Like little girls anywhere in the world, this
daughter had obviously gotten into her mother's makeup, and her
small hand had used it liberally.

But what took my breath away was her demeanor, the attitude
of her small body. As she stood biding her time and watching, her
posture, her position, the jaunty protrusion of her hip and turned out

---

65 Andrew Walls and Cathy Ross, Mission in the Twenty-First Century: Exploring the
Five Marks of Global Mission, (Maryknoll, NY: Orbis Books, 2008), 18.

foot were a chilling mirror image of her mom and thousands of other women who nightly line Falkland Road waiting for "customers." At four years of age, this little girl was already being groomed by the community of darkness for the community of darkness.

BACKGROUND

Yes, the community of darkness is very real, as is the community of light. Unfortunately for those of us born into individualistic cultures where individual identity and value take priority over group identity and value, we can easily underestimate the power of community—both for good and for evil. This cultural blind spot frequently leads to a highly individualistic theology, and as a result, shapes how we view and engage in compassion ministry and justice. In this chapter, we explore our individualism, its effect on our theology, and the important catalyst of community in life-changing compassion and justice.

In individualistic cultures such as those of traditional Anglo-America or much of Western Europe, identity, value, and achievement are defined individually from birth. Children are nurtured to grow toward the development of an individual identity and individual accomplishment. The proudest words of an American toddler are, "I can do it all by myself!" and that statement is applauded. Shaped by Erik Erikson's theory of healthy human development, the unquestioned goal is to mature the child and adolescent into an independent individual who can set personal goals and accomplish them through his or her own work and merit as much as possible. Western education has been based on

Erikson's theory and has perpetuated individualism globally with only limited question as to its universal validity until recent years.[66]

In cultures that prioritize independence and individualism, the family, group, and community are second in importance to the individual who has an assumed right to self-realization, self-fulfillment, and self-determination. Cross-cultural psychologist Alan Roland has termed this kind of individualized self that is so prevalent in traditional America and Northern Europe as the "I-self."[67]

Cultures with this kind of individualistic worldview, as documented in research by Geert Hofstede,[68] tend to participate in community to the extent that it furthers individual goals and desires. The unquestioned priority is to do what is good for the individual rather than what is good for the group.

Significantly, the "I-self" is not as common or valued by the majority of the non-Western world, which is increasingly the majority of the world's population. In much of Latin America, Africa, the Middle East, and Asia, and growing subcultures in America, children are nurtured from birth into a culture that places priority of the identity and good of the group, family, and community over that of the individual. From birth, a child's identity is defined and valued on the basis of belonging to a family, group, and community. Rather than healthy development being equated with a growing separate identity, independent from all others,

---

66 The fairly recent discipline of cross-cultural psychology provides great insight and information for those ministering across cultures, whether in other nations or within one's own increasingly multicultural ministry context. This section reflects research in that discipline with application made to Scripture and compassion ministries in cross-cultural contexts.

67 Alan Roland, *In Search of Self in India and Japan: Toward a Cross-Cultural Psychology* (Princeton, NJ: Princeton University Press, 1988).

68 Geert Hofstede, *Culture's Consequences: Comparing Values, Behaviors, Institutions, and Organizations Across Nations* (Thousand Oaks, CA: Sage Publications, 2001).

> The impact and significance of whether one's worldview is more individualistic or more group-oriented cannot be overestimated. It shapes every aspect of how we view life and expect to live it.

healthy human development is associated with how well the child learns to function in healthy relationships within the extended family and community. Independence is not the goal; interdependence is.[69] Roland refers to this kind of self-identity as the "we-self"—the person who puts the good and the interests of the group over those of the individual. This kind of collectivistic or community-based worldview, while not typically American, characterizes growing immigrant populations in America today (i.e., Latin, Southern Asian, Middle Eastern).

The impact and significance of whether one's worldview is more individualistic or more group-oriented cannot be overestimated. It shapes every aspect of how we view life and expect to live it. For the purposes of this study, more importantly, whether a person gains their identity and value as an individual or as part of a community influences how they view God, understand His Word, practice the community of faith, and interpret what it means to live life missionally as a follower of Jesus. It even influences how we view the needy, the poor, the enslaved, and how we view and practice compassion ministry to them.

---

69 Community-based compared to individualized cultures as nurtured from birth are effectively shared (almost without words) in the excellent documentary "Babies," http://www.focusfeatures.com/babies. It follows four babies and their immediate family in four cultures from pre-birth to their first birthday.

IMPLICATIONS FOR THE DECISION
TO FOLLOW JESUS

I first recall hearing the invitation of Jesus to follow Him when I was seven years of age. Sitting in my small home church beside my mom, I listened as a guest speaker proclaimed Jesus' life-changing invitation. "Whoever wants to be my disciple must deny themselves and take up their cross and follow me" (Matt. 16:24).

Without anyone knowing, quietly and deliberately, I made a decision as a small girl on a church pew that would change the course of my life and eternity. I decided to follow Jesus.

It has only been over years of ministry in different cultures that I've come to an important realization about my decision to follow Christ: it was not only a spiritual event but a cultural one. The fact that a little child of seven—especially a girl child!—would take a major decision alone (individually) without conferring with her parents and family is unthinkable in much of our world.

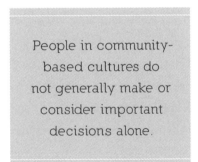

People in community-based cultures do not generally make or consider important decisions alone.

When I heard Jesus' invitation to follow Him, I heard Him inviting Beth, an individual child, separate and independent from all others, to follow Him. I knew He was asking me to deny myself— but that self was an independent, individual "I-self." (The fact that my father was from northern New England and my mother had good German background created in me an even stronger dose of that independent individualism that I would have to deny!)

In great contrast, in much of our world, Jesus' invitation to follow Him is heard differently. People in community-based cultures do not generally make or consider important decisions alone. Important decisions are contemplated and taken as an extended family because the outcomes of the decision will impact the family, either positively or negatively. In that majority-world context, it is considered selfish for a member of the family to take a decision alone when it will impact the whole family and community.

Secondly, individuals in community-based cultures hear Jesus' condition about "denying" themselves to follow Him through a different lens. While I anticipated denying the individual Beth, an "I-self" separate from all others, people in community cultures know they will be paying an extremely different price to follow Jesus. They will be denying a "we-self" identity—the family and community with which their identity is inextricably intertwined. From a community culture perspective, they will be betraying everyone with whom their identity is connected from birth to death. In effect, the price for following Jesus is not infrequently the loss of family, relationships, economic resources, and even marriage and children. No wonder the "we-self" individual may contemplate the decision to follow Jesus for months if not years. This is most often the inevitable costly spiritual journey of those from other religious traditions whom we invite to follow Jesus.

This reality becomes soberly clear in India when a new believer coming from a Hindu or Muslim background decides to follow Jesus and be baptized in water. The step to public baptism is not an easy one nor is it taken lightly. The new follower of Jesus knows that this action of obedience to Jesus also declares publicly that they have chosen to disengage from their community of birth and their cultural religious identity to become a part of a new community and a new religion. Baptism is a sober moment. New believers who are denying the "we-self" know they now face the beginning of ostracization, deep loss, and often persecution. The loss of one's family and community is considered the deepest possible tragedy one can endure—the death of the "we-self."

THE IMPLICATIONS OF COMMUNITY IN GOD'S MISSION

When we bring this understanding of community cultures to God's Word and engagement in God's compassion, it provides fresh insight into God's mission and those men and women He uses to accomplish it. For example, the historical call of Abram described in Genesis 12:1–5 is much more than the story of Abram, the individual Father of faith and rugged individualist missionary:

> The LORD had said to Abram, "Go from your country, your people and your father's household (strong community) to the land that I will show you.
>
> I will make you into a great nation (a new community/ corporate promise)
>
> and I will bless you (a personal promise);
>
> I will make your name great, and you will be a blessing (a personal promise).
>
> I will bless those who bless you, and whoever curses you I will curse;
>
> And all peoples on earth will be blessed through you (a community, corporate promise).

So Abram went, as the LORD had told him; and Lot went with him. Abram was seventy-five-years old when he set out from Haran. He took his wife, Sarai, his nephew Lot, all the possessions they had accumulated and the people they had acquired in Haran . . . (individual and community obedience).

The exciting truth in this passage is that God's call and promise to Abram had both individual and community components. God was asking this man to tear himself away from his cultural, ancestral community, with its security and status, to birth in him a new community that God was instituting through him: the people of God. But the depth of sacrifice and obedience this required of Abram can only be appreciated when we understand the strength and security of his "we-self" identity. On the other hand, it helps those of us with a highly individual lens to appreciate that God's covenant with Abram would replace his loss of an earthly community with a spiritual community—the people of God. And in the process, Abram the individual servant of God would be blessed as well.

Interestingly, we find a parallel passage with the same spiritual truth in the New Testament in a different time and place. In 1 Peter 2:9–10, the writer proclaims to believers:

But you are a chosen people, a royal priesthood, a holy nation, God's special possession (community), that you may declare the praises of him who called you out of darkness into his wonderful light (a corporate mission). Once you were not a people, but now you are the people of God (community identity); once you had not received mercy, but now you have received mercy.

And the community or people of God birthed out of the Abrahamic covenant and recognized by Peter continues to this day!

EXPECTATIONS FOR BEING PART OF THE COMMUNITY OF FAITH

Whether an individual's worldview is individualistic (I-self) or more group-oriented (we-self) strongly shapes his or her expectations of how families and communities function. How a new follower of Jesus expects the "family of God" or "community of faith" to function is no exception.

For example, it is safe to say that when men and women come to Christ in evangelical churches in America, they typically have modest expectations from the church family in which they make that decision. Why? Because in our larger culture, extended families tend to have loose relationships with family members and have little responsibility for each other as adults. Frequently, family members do not live in close proximity, and if they do, family members may come together for meals and holidays only. Economic, emotional, and physical independence is valued. Interdependence is not the goal. Dependence is considered unhealthy. Everyone should be able to "stand on their own two feet." And, we think, surely God has the same perspective.

As a result, that kind of "I-self" family community is carried over into how we do church "family." We do well at eating together for special events and celebrating holidays. But, in actuality, when it comes to day-to-day, week-to-week life, members of the local community of faith are expected to make it on their own as much as possible. Again, in spite of our high view of Scripture, our cultural value on individualism and independence clouds our understanding and practice of New Testament teaching about the interdependent body of Christ described by Paul in 1 Corinthians 12. We are quite content to hug one another on Sunday morning, say we love one another, but have little to no responsibility for one another or interaction until the next Sunday.

But what about the person from a strong community-based culture (i.e., Latin, East Indian, Asian, Middle Eastern) who comes to the same American evangelical church, hears the invitation of Jesus to follow Him, and takes that life-changing decision? When leaders say, "We love you," and "We are your brothers and sisters in Christ," members of strong community cultures hear those words with different expectations than the Anglo-American pastor or well-meaning church member intends. Much to the church staff's surprise, the new believer may end up at the church office the next Monday morning, desperate for economic, emotional, and spiritual help— in that order. If they have been disowned by their human family and community for following Jesus, they desperately need to come into a new "family" of God: a faith community that functions fully as family. If the local church is "family" in the best biblical sense, the new believer will be welcomed and strengthened on the faith journey for the days, months, and years to come. If the American church is simply a group of independent, individualized Christians meeting at the same place at the same time on Sunday morning,

> We are quite content to hug one another on Sunday morning, say we love one another, but have little to no responsibility for one another or interaction until the next Sunday.

the new believer out of a strong community culture may not survive beyond the first weeks of spiritual new life. On the other hand, if the church in a community-based culture leads a visiting, rugged individualist to Christ, the strong interdependent community of faith may cause the new culturally-independent believer to feel overwhelmed and smothered by relational expectations!

HOW DOES THIS MATTER TO HUMAN NEED AND COMPASSION MINISTRY?

By this time, I'm quite sure readers are wondering how in the world understanding our personal individualistic or community-based cultural worldview is pertinent to a book about a courageous and compassionate response to our violent, unjust Isaiah 59 world! Let's just do justice!

Let's look briefly at some of the effects of our individualism on our theology that form the basis for our compassionate practice of justice:

1. Christians in "I-self" cultures tend to place priority on individual salvation rather than on people coming to Christ as families or communities. The old gospel song "Just Jesus and me . . ." is closer to our theology than Joshua's declaration, "But as for me and my household, we will serve the LORD" (Josh. 24:15).

2. For independent "I-selfs", a personal relationship with Jesus takes far greater priority in our faith walk than relationships with others—even in the community of faith. (For interdependent "we-self" cultures, believers would have difficulty biblically

and practically separating one's personal relationship to Jesus from how it is integrated in relationships within the family of God. Faith is both personal and corporate.)

3. In individualistic cultures, believers can view participating in the community of faith/local church as optional rather than a necessary part of their Christian faith and spiritual formation.

4. The "family of God" is more of a concept than a practical reality.

5. The call of God to mission and ministry is viewed as largely personal and individual rather than a group or community mission. Individual calls to ministry and personal visions are assumed to take priority over those of the team or group.

Flowing out of these perspectives come corollary assumptions about those without Christ who need salvation, healing, and transformation. The individual needs Jesus and is therefore approached individually, with secondary attention to the community context and its effect on the individual's decision.

Our prayers and intercession are generally focused on individuals who need salvation, deliverance, and healing. We try to ignore the community of darkness and related systems of evil from which the individual must come.

When faced with great human need, we tend to think of responding to help as individuals rather than communities, groups, or teams. (The work of Convoy of Hope is an inspiring exception to the traditional individualized approach. It focuses on community and individuals simultaneously.[70]) Some of these implications of our cultural individualism or collectivism might best be seen in an all-too-frequent real-life scenario.

THE INTRUSION OF CONFLICTING REALITIES IN DOING JUSTICE

An American college student, Lori has become aware of the tragedy of global sex trafficking. She is a passionate Christian and has a growing desire to help trafficking victims find freedom. Her compassion is strong and her intentions sincere.

LORI'S REALITY

In doing internet research, Lori connects with an organization claiming to rescue trafficking victims in an Asian country. Short-term ministry trips are offered in which young people can travel to Asia for two weeks and help free prostituted women and children. The college student fervently prays about going and raises several thousand dollars in order to take the two-week summer trip. People who love and respect her pledge to help in her worthy cause. All in her church and circle of friends want to help sex slaves find freedom and hope in Jesus Christ.

LORI'S ASSUMPTIONS ABOUT THE REALITY OF THE LIVES OF SEX SLAVES

Lori's reality is based on several significant assumptions:

---

70   See www.convoyofhope.org.

1. All sex slaves want to be free—by our definition of freedom.

2. Language differences will not really matter when we do good.

3. Sex slaves have some degree of individual autonomy to make individual decisions about their lives.

4. Once a sex slave is physically out of slavery, she is free to make good choices.

5. If a young woman in slavery prays the "sinner's prayer" with Lori, she is a Christian, and everything is changed.

REALITY AS EXPERIENCED BY WOMEN IN SEXUAL SLAVERY

The women whom Lori will meet on her trip have a different reality, however:

1. Women don't necessarily want to be free from sexual slavery if that is all they have known—especially if they have been exploited since childhood. Often they will settle for the horror of the known rather than the fear of the unknown.

2. Chances are the impoverished women Lori will meet don't understand her English. However, in many cultures, people will graciously smile and nod so as not to embarrass a foreign guest. Nodding

heads and smiles may indicate kind hospitality, not necessarily understanding or salvation.

3. Many sex slaves in Asia were born into community-based cultures. When taken into slavery, they were forced to trade one community for another. The community of prostitution may be all they know. As a result, they are not used to making individual decisions and are afraid to do so—especially without relationships and trust.

4. For many women and girls in the world of sexual exploitation, there are only two groups of people: the exploited and the exploiters. When they see Lori coming from America, they will silently be assessing into which category (or community) to place her. Frequently, in the community of exploitation, the only way for a prostituted woman to escape a life of exploitation is to become an exploiter of other women herself. That is often how women become madams. If they conclude Lori is not being exploited, they will privately wonder how she might exploit them (i.e., use their photos or stories to raise money which they will never see?).

5. When prostituted women and children realize Lori is only there for two weeks, why would they take a risky, frightening decision to try and escape their violent community of darkness? Unless there is a respected local group in the community with which Lori is working that will help them long-term, why would exploited women risk beatings and violence

for interaction with a foreigner—while Lori goes safely back home to the U.S. or Europe? Whom can they trust? How can they trust?

Questions for Reflection and Discussion

1. What are some cultural and theological assumptions that lie behind Lori's assumptions in going to Asia on a short-term ministry trip? In what areas are her assumptions biblical? In what areas are her assumptions possibly biblically inaccurate or culturally inappropriate?

2. There are some areas of disconnect and potential misunderstanding between Lori's reality and the reality of the prostituted women she will meet. What adjustments could Lori make in her approach to her short-term compassion trip to bring freedom and an opportunity for a new life more effectively to those she will meet?

3. In order to make those adjustments in expectations and her actions, what will be Lori's greatest personal challenges, and why?

4. Discuss the ways Lori's approach is influenced by her individualistic culture and theology. In what ways are you challenged to rethink your compassionate expectations and actions?

THE COMMUNITY FACTOR IN
HUMAN NEED AND INJUSTICE

We are bombarded with compelling media images almost every day: a child in poverty, a person dying of AIDS-related illness, a drug addict, or a child victim of prostitution. We are both drawn and repelled by the pain, the suffering, the injustice to the person. It's all too easy to miss the fact that each one who so desperately needs Jesus and compassionate help is embedded

> It's all too easy to miss the fact that each one who so desperately needs Jesus and compassionate help is embedded in a community.

in a community. Poverty, HIV/AIDS, drug addiction, and sexual exploitation all occur in a tangible context, a setting, a community. They generally do not occur in isolation although that may appear to be the case.

On January 12, 2010, the small Caribbean island of Haiti experienced a devastating earthquake that left an estimated 100 to 150 thousand people dead and a heartbreaking percentage of the total population homeless and desperate for aid.[71] The world viewed the news in horror, responding generously and sacrificially to bring relief to the hurting Haitian people. But complicating relief efforts, the natural disaster occurred to an island nation with a history of corruption, exploitation, and demonic spiritual activity. Four years after the earthquake and worldwide compassionate response to help, the cultural, political, and spiritual realities of

---

71 Wikipedia, "2010 Haiti Earthquake," http://en.wikipedia.org/wiki/2010_Haiti_earth-quake.

Haiti as a context for compassion have crippled the effectiveness of redevelopment for the impoverished Haitian people. The community context for compassion is never neutral. It is a reality of which God-inspired compassionate action must be aware and sensitively prepared to engage. It has been our observation that compassion and justice efforts that are highly individualized and undervalue the power of local community rarely succeed in making lasting change in people's lives.

- The child who is fed will have to deal with the community of hungry children around him who were not fed.

- The women dying from AIDS-related tuberculosis may well have several infected, malnourished children lying on the floor of her earthen hut nearby. What about them?

- The drug addict needing help with addiction is hopelessly enslaved as long as he or she remains in the community controlled by drug dealers.

- Little girls like the one I saw in the red-light district church are not alone. They live daily in a literal city of prostitution and darkness, among tens of thousands of enslaved women and children. The pressure to conform is unrelenting and virtually impossible to escape.

Yes, Jesus came to bring new life, healing, and good purposes to each person described above! We must be aware on a practical and spiritual level that we are not only challenging the darkness of bondage in the lives of *individuals*, but we as the community of faith must also prayerfully challenge the *community* of darkness where evil reigns.

IN COMMUNITY, PRESENCE IS EVERYTHING

Traditionally, many of us Pentecostals have tried our best to keep our distance from the community of darkness while trying to obey God's mission to reach the lost and enslaved from the safety of our churches. Given the depravity, violence, and demonic power that characterize the community of darkness in our Isaiah 59 world, this avoidance and desire of people of faith to stay as far away as possible is understandable. But how can we fulfill Jesus' Luke 4:18 mandate to set captives free from inside church walls when the captives cannot come out of their place of slavery to receive Christ's freedom?

Thank God, we have exemplary and inspiring twenty-first century examples of men and women of faith in our generation who take God's compassionate heart for those in the community of darkness seriously. Ambika Pandey is one such woman.

Ambika was born into a religious family in South India. After graduating from college, she became employed by a company in which the manager and his wife were dedicated followers of Jesus. Through their friendship, witness, prayer, and a miraculous revelation of Jesus as the One who is light, Ambika was powerfully transformed and filled with the Holy Spirit.

Feeling led to prepare for ministry, Ambika determined to go to Bible college. There she met the young man who would later become her husband. Upon graduation, they went to another city in India, where they would pastor a church and she would eventually become a professor at a local Bible college. But something else was happening in Ambika's heart. She began to have dreams of working with women enslaved in prostitution. The dreams were real but troubling for a woman from her background. To have anything to do with "these kinds of women" would be taboo for a good, moral Indian woman. Any involvement with them would bring questions regarding her own reputation and honor. And yet, the dreams persisted.

One day Ambika learned of an opportunity to help with a red-light district Sunday school that Mother Teresa's sisters had started. When her local Assembly of God church was approached about this need, no one knew that God had already been preparing the heart of a Bible college professor and pastor's wife through dreams. Ambika stepped up, shared her burden with tears, and begin courageous weekly visits into the red-light district to work with the children of prostituted women. For several years, this woman of God, mother, and wife prayer-walked obediently into a world of sexual violence and tangible evil to be with little children whom Jesus loves deeply. Through her presence, prayer, her teaching of God's Word, and her faithful love for them, the children grew to love "Auntie Ambika." Mothers hardened by a life of sexual violence came to respect and trust this woman of God.

Only after several years of sacrificially modeling Jesus' incarnational ministry did Ambika and her staff finally have the opportunity to help the first children leave the red-light district. Trust is hard to earn among those whose trust has been constantly betrayed. But what a day that was! Today, there are eighteen young girls in the safety of an aftercare home who know Jesus, love Him, and are finding healing from the abuses of their pasts. There are now eighteen women who came out of the brothels for vocational training to be able to leave the district and begin a new life. The vocational center has become a church in function where women living in great darkness are welcome to walk in the door, begin training, and begin to hear about Jesus. In this unassuming place, contemporary Mary Magdalenes are loved, come to know Jesus, and learn to follow Him.

What if Ambika had avoided the community of darkness? What if she had stopped going where her life was threatened and she had to push her way past hundreds of lustful men bargaining for sex? What if, after a year, she had concluded it wasn't worth the risk, the discomfort, the chilling intimidation of demonic power?

Thank God for the Ambika Pandeys in the community of light today who have heard God's call to leave the comfort, convenience, and safety of the church to go into the community of darkness to help captives find freedom. They know that the presence of anointed men and women of God is essential to help those in bondage find genuine freedom and deliverance.

THE LOCAL COMMUNITY OF FAITH AS ULTIMATE COMPASSIONATE STRATEGY

Individual compassionate and just acts are commended repeatedly in Scripture, indicating God's desire and approval. Conversely, those who do not do them reap God's displeasure.

- He who is kind to the poor lends to the LORD, and he will reward him for what he has done (Prov. 19:17).

- Whoever shuts their ears to the cry of the poor will also cry out and not be answered (Prov. 21:13).

- Defend the weak and the fatherless; uphold the cause of the poor and oppressed (Ps. 82:3).

- Whoever oppresses the poor shows contempt for their Maker, but whoever is kind to the needy honors God (Prov. 14:31).

- And if anyone gives even a cup of cold water to one of these little ones who is my disciple, truly I tell you, that person will certainly not lose their reward (Matt. 10:42).

> The ultimate expression of Christ's life-changing compassion can only be realized, multiplied, and sustained toward God's ultimate purposes through individuals working together in the local community of faith.

But individual believers doing compassion alone are only part of the implementation of God's purposes. The ultimate expression of Christ's life-changing compassion can only be realized, multiplied, and sustained toward God's ultimate purposes through individuals working together in the local community of faith. Anything less than this is weakened in its holistic capacity to bring salvation, healing, discipleship, restoration, and the fulfillment of God's purposes in the lives of the poor, the exploited, the captive, and the oppressed!

Let's look at some specific ways in which the local community of faith is the unique and essential foundation for transformational compassion.

1. The local community of faith is a strong base for intercessory prayer. Compassionate acts alone are not transformational. They must be bathed in intercession before, during, and after—especially when dealing with those enslaved in spiritual, mental, physical, and emotional bondage. (See chapter 10, "How Can We Help ... Besides Pray?" The Strategy of Intercession.")

2. The local community of faith is the *only* source for faith-based outreach workers, staff, and volunteers for compassion ministries. Think about that. Obvious, but is it overlooked? Compassionate acts are being performed by good people globally all the time. But compassionate ministry that brings spiritual as well as physical restoration leading to a new life occurs only through people of faith.

3. The local community of faith is the long-term source of resources (both human and financial) to support sustainable compassion ministries in the community. While support from national or international agencies can be effective in launching compassion ministries, it is difficult to sustain long-term. Foreign workers eventually go home. Nonresident nationals go back and forth to their new home outside their nation of birth. Funding agencies eventually take up a new project or cause. Local financial responsibility enhances the sustainability of compassion ministries and the feeling of ownership by the local body of Christ.

4. The leadership of the local community of faith can provide accountability, legitimacy, and strength to compassion ministries. Ideally, local church leadership has an integrated vision for missional compassionate ministries in the local church that are a healthy, biblical part of—not separate from—proclamation and discipleship. Also, justice initiatives and their leaders may appear impressive from a distance and in promotional materials, yet have a different reputation in their local community and nation. A respected local national church can verify the legitimacy and integrity of local initiatives or raise concerns that need to be addressed. Anything can look impressive from a distance, with enough good marketing.

5. Most importantly, the local community of faith must become the "family" that loves, supports, mentors, and disciples those coming to Christ out of poverty and bondage. One individual can be greatly used of God in compassion ministry—but an individual cannot fulfill the spiritual function in the life of new believers as the "community of faith" in which God intends the new believer to belong.

Compassion ministries that are not connected to a healthy local church are started by good people with good intentions. But the potential for healing and life change in victims of injustice is diminished and even aborted in short-term compassionate fixes by individuals who work alone.

CONCLUSION

Remember Lori, who went on a two-week visit to an Asian country to help rescue women in sexual slavery? If her team is in dialogue and collaboration with a local, respected community of faith in the city where they will minister, their compassionate initiatives will have the following advantages and potential for long-term life change in prostituted women:

- Local church leadership and/or believers can provide guidance for Lori and her team in the community to assess ahead of time where and how they can best minister to local women in slavery. Preparation can be made for the most effective outreach.

- If Lori encounters a prostituted girl or woman who genuinely wants help, people from the local church who are involved in social work, law enforcement, legal counsel, and medical services will be able to follow up with the girl after Lori leaves. Godly women in the church who have spiritual authority to deal with demonic power will be available to help with needs for deliverance. This will all be done in the prostituted woman's language, which is essential.

- After Lori leaves the country, women believers in the local church can become friends and ongoing spiritual mentors to the women with whom Lori has connected. For those coming out of bondage, healing is most often a messy journey of spiritual battle and faith rather than a life-changing moment. It requires

patience and strength, sometimes 24/7 for months,
even years. God can use Lori as a catalyst while
there, but the local church will be there long-term to
help the women continue their journey to new life.

And remember our hero, Ambika Pandey, in India? Her
ministry to prostituted women and children is not a solo performance.
She is supported, advised by, and accountable to a board of leaders
from the local church and community. The Assemblies of God
Mission Church under the leadership of Dr. Ivan Satyavrata
supports her with intercession, office space, and finances. Ambika
has a wonderful team of ladies who work with her as staff. In the
community of faith on Sunday, she is a fellow follower of Jesus
receiving mutual ministry from brothers and sisters in Christ. That
is why Ambika is so strong—even on the most difficult of days.
Long-term, life-changing courageous compassion flows out of the
God-ordained strengths of the local community of faith.

SUGGESTED LEARNING EXPERIENCE

Activity: "Community of Darkness, Community of Light" (See appendix D).

FOR FURTHER STUDY

- Hellerman, Joseph H. "A Family Affair: What Would the Church Look Like If It Put *We* before *Me?*" *Christianity Today* 54, no. 5 (May 28, 2010).

- Hofstede, Geert. *Culture's Consequences: Comparing Values, Behaviors, Institutions, and Organizations Across Nations.* Thousand Oaks, CA: Sage Publications, 2001.

- Jayson, Sharon. (2012). "What's on Americans' Minds? Increasingly, 'Me': Innovative Look at Digitized Books Reveals a Realm of Individualism." *USA Today*, July 11, 2012.

CHAPTER 9

CREATIVE COMPASSION: FORGING A NEW PATH

BY REBECCA GRANT SHULTS

I was born in the rain.
My mummy loved me very much
So she sent me away.
I was only three years old
She worked under red lights
Worked to pay a strange family
To raise and keep and feed me
Little girl sleeping on the kitchen floor
So cold in the winter, so hungry all year.
One year, two years, three years
Year after year, so scared of this Auntie
Burns on my skin and beatings.
Three years, four years, five years
My mummy sent gifts
Money for a good school and clothes
Auntie took everything away
Little girl, starving, asking Auntie for food
She shoves chili in my eyes and says,
"Later, later, little girl. Go to sleep."
Year after year, six years of torture

Mummy never knew

I could never tell

So long was this torture, how could I forgive?

For six more years I tried . . .

So long it took to forgive

Today I look out from my window

Rain falls fresh like joy

Falling, falling from the sky

WRITTEN BY SATEEN, A YOUNG GIRL IN A

PROJECT RESCUE HOME OF HOPE

"Our first-born daughter, Rebecca, was three weeks old when I realized I had given birth to a strong-willed child. By the time she was three, she was also extremely creative and gifted. From the time Becca could write, she created little books and illustrated them by the hour. As the daughter of traveling evangelists, she spent endless time in services, airplanes, and restaurants day after day. She learned to spend those hours reading, writing, journaling, and drawing. I have a gallery of treasured art done on restaurant placemats from around the world, given lovingly by our creative daughter over her growing-up years. Rebecca is now a wife, mother, and coworker in Project Rescue. One of our greatest joys has been to walk with her as she discovered God's unique and creative call on her life. As Rebecca's story illustrates in the following pages, there is a place for the arts in courageous, holistic, life-changing compassion. Her journey is best told in her own irrepressible words."

INTRODUCTORY COMMENTS BY BETH GRANT

THE BIRTH OF A CREATIVE CALL TO HEALING

I was sixteen when I was first taken through the red-light district of Bombay. It was monsoon season and the rain had flooded the night streets of Kamathapura, where a hundred thousand women were forced to solicit customers in rooms, in cages, on the street. The flooding slowed our vehicle, as we inched painfully through a sea of girls, young and old, standing, waiting, with pimps watching close by. I looked into the eyes of girls my age and younger through the windows and saw the most harrowing blank stares—emptiness. These souls had lost their will and identity. They had ceased to hope.

> I looked into the eyes of girls my age and younger through the windows and saw the most harrowing blank stares—emptiness.

Minutes later we drove to a tiny apartment where a dozen ladies awaited us. They received us with warmth, and we sat down on the concrete living room floor as they served us *chai*. We chatted casually, and then the girls began to share what they had planned for us to hear; how God had rescued them out of slavery in the red-light district and given them new hope. A few ladies had only recently been rescued, but they already wanted to talk about how good God had been to them. I have never seen such a contrast: from empty eyes on the street, to joyful eyes in that first Project Rescue home with Bombay Teen Challenge.

That night I realized for the first time that I serve the only God who says that every girl in the world has eternal value and possesses a destiny as His daughter, no matter where she was born or what she has done. In a culture that tells every girl her only chance at a future is her father's good name and her virginity, my God is the only one who offers new life to girls who have neither. My God not only brings physical freedom to those in slavery, but spiritual and emotional freedom. The hopeless faces in the district that night stuck with me, and I continued to dream of those rescued who needed to heal. I instinctively knew that this healing process must be a slow journey, and I hoped that one day I would be a part of it.

This visit to Bombay in 1997 was my first experience of the work my parents had helped to birth. In the years following, they founded six more Project Rescue ministries with other colleagues in other cities, and the aftercare homes were called "Homes of Hope." I frequently listened to Project Rescue's progress as more and more women entered into new, life-giving community, but as I headed back to the US in 1999 for university, I wondered how I could ever be a part of the lives of these women and children. As I wrestled with degree options, Mom told me, "Do what you love to do and let God figure out what to do with it."

I began university, majoring in drama-speech education. As it turned out, I was a lousy actress, but I had a knack for directing and scriptwriting. This pushed me to explore ways to create social change through original drama. When I began student teaching, I quickly realized that teaching high school was not my calling. In order to figure out a next step for my foggy future, I began a master's degree in theatre arts at Missouri State University. What I didn't realize at the time was how necessary my skills in classroom management, special education, and lesson planning would one day be with trauma survivors!

It was in the second year of my graduate work that I began studying how artists—dancers, writers, and visual artists—used their art form to bring healing to survivors of trauma. Creative artists around the globe use the arts to help children express their hurt, to help communities face social challenges, and to give a voice to the voiceless. I explored hundreds of possible uses for theatre and script writing to help the hurting, but I could find no one using creativity for healing in a faith-based setting.

It wasn't until a lunch date with my mom during my final semester that my worlds collided. As she shared about a new curriculum she was developing for Project Rescue staff, I said, "I want to work with Project Rescue! I could use the arts!" She looked at me, probably amused at my own look of astonishment and said, "Of course you can. Why don't you apply?" To my amazement, there was no longer anything standing in my way of working with Project Rescue—I was finishing my education with no school debt, obligations, or boyfriend, and I now possessed tools to bring healing to survivors of trauma!

I spent my last semester in grad school designing and implementing a pilot project for "healing through the arts" with teen foster care survivors of sexual abuse. Together, ten girls and I wrote, choreographed, and assembled an original performance to share their stories, their dreams, and their own newly perceived authority to choose their own future. It ended with a hip-hop dance to Destiny's Child's "Survivor," choreographed and performed by the girls. The audience of carefully selected family, friends, caseworkers and teachers sat in rapt attention and tears. At the end one girl's mother—a frail, haggard woman juggling a couple of toddlers by her side—came up and told her daughter, "I never knew how I hurt you." She had dropped her daughter off with social services several times during her young life, leaving her for up to a year at a time. It was a heartbreaking, life-changing moment I'll never forget.

Nine years after my first encounter with rescued girls in India, it was time to embark on my own journey to India. I had never felt a special calling to India, despite my parents' thirty-plus years of focus there. However, I did have a calling to bring healing, and the door to India was open. If I had known all that lay ahead, I'm sure I would have been too overwhelmed to go! Nevertheless, a one-year commitment turned into five years of healing through the arts with Project Rescue, and ultimately the development of a technique called Rescue Arts.

> There is no true healing without Jesus. He is the God who promises healing when we ask.

One thought is nagging at me as I write. It is the greatest revelation I have had since finishing graduate work and embarking on thousands of Rescue Arts sessions with trauma survivors on three continents: There is no true healing without Jesus. He is the God who promises healing when we ask. I have personally seen hundreds of women and children find emotional healing, a new identity, and forgiveness for all those who have hurt them. Their history would seem to make this impossible. While we employ the arts (creativity and expression) and ensemble work as tools for healing, we can do little without a loving God who speaks truth into broken hearts that will hear.

THE COMPASSIONATE ARTIST:
A CALL TO HANDS-ON HEALING

There is a stereotype of the narcissistic artist that occasionally rings true. But I would like to propose a new stereotype—that of the *compassionate* artist. What I have found in my travels are many talented, creative individuals with a compassionate heart for the hurting and a desire for a technique in order to do something meaningful. Whether we dance, photograph, or sing, the One who designed our creativity also planned creative ways for us to bring miraculous change. Some of us have a passion for community social change, and others for change in the individual survivor of abuse. I have seen the arts do both—when coupled with the Holy Spirit—to much avail.

There is an important difference between *advocacy* through the arts and *healing* through the arts. While the concept of healing through the arts was unfamiliar to me when I began, it is quite a popular field of study now. I am approached in hundreds of cities around the world by individuals searching for the right internship or program through which they can use their art form to bring healing. Many of these individuals desire to *write* or to *perform*. During my studies, I originally thought this might be the only role I could play in the lives of trafficking survivors—to write and to direct productions about them—to *advocate* through the performing arts. This type of advocacy has actually become quite common today, and there are countless groups promoting awareness of the traumatized across the globe.

However, as important as advocacy is, it does not bring healing through the arts to those who are hurting most. I'm thankful for the opportunity to work directly with many sexual trauma survivors,

> But it is an indescribable joy to watch a survivor finally discover God's truth in her story, her new and eternal identity, and her dreams through creative means.

to learn how best to help them find healing, and to develop an approach to bring healing through the arts. Working directly with survivors is less glamorous, more complex and involved, and takes longer than promoting awareness about them. But it is an indescribable joy to watch a survivor finally discover God's truth in her story, her new and eternal identity, and her dreams through creative means. When she owns her own story and discovers her own voice, she discovers a power she never knew she had. No moment is more victorious than the moment when she discovers the ability to choose who she will be and express it to an audience of her choice. It's for that moment that I have worked to develop a responsible method of healing through the arts.

I pray that in the years to come Christian artists will forge new roads to the brokenhearted, and use creative means to facilitate lasting healing and change. With both the Ultimate Healer and the Ultimate Creator within arm's reach, we should be creating the most true, profound art and reaching those who are hurting in the most tangible, creative ways possible.

INFLUENCES ON AND DEVELOPMENT OF RESCUE ARTS

Seven years of leading interns, teams, training events, and ongoing work with trauma survivors has fine-tuned my work in Rescue Arts.

In the journey that formed Rescue Arts, I developed a number of non-negotiables. First, I discovered that healing did not happen without discipleship—a clear understanding within the individual of her value and identity in Christ—and that discipleship was not sufficient without ample opportunity and atmosphere for healing.

Second, in adapting to the Indian culture, I became committed to a community-based approach to healing. Ensemble work is a critical and ongoing part of Rescue Arts projects because it can strengthen participants' relationships with one another and with long-term caregivers. When trauma survivors are rescued out of a *strong community* of bondage, a committed, hope-filled, tight *community of faith* is needed to walk out the journey to healing.

> Art and dance became critical components to facilitate healing with all sexual trauma survivors, but especially with those who could not write or had experienced sexual abuse at a very young age.

Third, I incorporated more dance, songwriting, and visual/tactile art than I originally began with, partly because in India everyone loves to dance. While living in one Home of Hope and leading a project with a group of teenage girls, I realized that half the group was not showing up to sessions solely focused on writing, so I started spreading the word throughout the morning, "This afternoon we're going to learn a new dance!" and everyone would show up to dance. Dance became a way to release endorphins, create a fun, nonthreatening environment, and get emotions flowing for times of writing and creativity.

Fourth, when girls could not write, they could still paint and collage powerfully. This was especially important when the trauma they had experienced occurred at an early age before language acquisition. In these cases, they were often initially unable to express their trauma in words. Hence, art and dance became critical components to facilitate healing with all sexual trauma survivors, but especially with those who could not write or had experienced sexual abuse at a very young age.

These concepts of ensemble work, the use of multiple tactile and kinesthetic creative forms, and hand-in-hand healing and discipleship have had an enormous impact in the shaping of Rescue Arts.

SARITA'S STORY

Sarita was born in a tiny brothel where her mother was forced to receive customers into the eighth month of her pregnancy, and again one month after Sarita was born. Sarita was fed milk with alcohol to help her sleep under her mother's bed during working hours. Occasionally, when no one was paying attention, Sarita was pulled aside and used by customers, along with her brother. Sarita's brother, Sahil, was made into a eunuch very early in life, and by the age of sixteen she watched him become a prostitute at the Hindu temple steps. At the age of twelve, Sarita overheard her mother making plans to sell her to a bar owner, and she ran away. Sarita met a Project Rescue outreach worker that very day, who welcomed her into a Project Rescue Home of Hope.

Sarita's *greatest* needs are food, shelter, education, and medical care. Yes! But what can help Sarita's heart to heal from years of trauma, rejection, and fear? There are organizations making documentaries about girls like Sarita and artists creating paintings of them. These projects may raise funds to feed and educate Sarita, which is critical, but consider the artist who teaches Sarita to express, to process healthily, and to grow closer to her community of faith. This artist has the most direct impact on the survivor. This is the impact of bringing healing through the arts.

I first lived in Sarita's Home of Hope for five weeks. For three weeks of sessions, Sarita came to the upstairs room where we danced, wrote our stories, and made visual art. She had little to contribute and said that she had nothing to share. Sarita watched as her sisters expressed sorrow and fears they had never shared before. She noticed that in this carefully crafted atmosphere of safety and creativity, no one was criticized or shamed. Every story was received and believed. Story-tellers were affirmed, lies were debunked, and truth—eternal truth—was spoken over those who shared. After three long weeks, Sarita broke. First she informed me she would no longer come to sessions. When I pursued her to her room one afternoon and pressed, she began pouring out tears of fear, shame, and vulnerability. She shared the story she had never wanted to share, that had been hidden for five years from her "family" in this Home of Hope.

Two weeks later Sarita stood with eleven Project Rescue sisters and was the only one to tell her story so directly, so courageously. Between ensemble-created dance, script, and art, Sarita shared the pain that her caregivers and sisters had never heard. She destroyed the bondage of silence for both herself and the girls around her. Her heart began to mend through the power of trust and the arts.

RESCUE ARTS: THE FRAMEWORK

Rescue Arts is a framework for expression, processing, and relational development. Rescue Arts uses *any* creative medium to:

1. Provide a safe place for trauma survivors to express through creative means, based on their own choice of content;

2. Process what they have created both introspectively and collectively; and

3. Work together to further develop or perform their creation, fostering relational development, trust, and healthy attachment.

This is a simple and necessary framework that gives the facilitator the freedom to adapt his or her art form(s) to the needs of the group, the timeframe, and the setting. While there may be a performance, this is not a necessary part of the healing process, nor is it the focus of Rescue Arts.

LESSONS LEARNED

I would like to share lessons that I learned in my endeavors to bring healing through the arts with women and children in Project Rescue. Following are a few principles for practice in facilitating healing through the arts.

1. *Follow best practices.* Care for survivors of trauma has been done before—both well and harmfully. Professionals have

established "best practices"—the wisest and most effective mode of operation—and training and mentorship are critical in hands-on work with survivors. During the crash-course of a first year serving Project Rescue in India, I learned to follow the wisdom of experts in working with survivors of sexual exploitation (a great source for this is the Hands That Heal Curriculum, eds. Grant and Hudlin). It is critical that we enter into relationship with trauma survivors responsibly.

2. *The greatest factor for emotional health in a trauma survivor's life is attachment to a long-term caregiver* (Goldin and Hughes, 2012). If I spend one month or even five years with survivors, I am not the relationship they need most for healing. It is the local, committed caregiver (whether a parent, foster parent, or aftercare staff) to whom the survivor must attach. Therefore, when I facilitate the arts for healing, my primary goal is to draw survivors closer to one another and to their community. In order to do this, I often a) encourage survivors to share their story with their caregiver—not just with me; b) request that a trusted caregiver be present during our sessions; and c) facilitate creative opportunities for survivors to interact with and bond with one another and caregivers. Instead of drawing a survivor closer to myself, I step back to allow the long-term healing to continue with caregivers who will walk with her indefinitely.

3. *Prayerfully discern how much (or little) a survivor needs to share.* For a trauma survivor, telling her personal narrative can be a powerful tool for healing, helping her to gain a

sense of control over the memory (instead of the other way around). However, telling too much of the story at once, or in a group setting that is not confidential and emotionally supportive, or in a way in which she feels pressured to share difficult details over and over can intensify the impact of the traumatic memory. A good approach is to refrain from directing which aspects of their narrative survivors will share, allowing freedom over content, but with sufficient boundaries in the assignment to make "success" achievable (such as, "draw an image of a positive memory from your childhood"). Instead of prying out a child's full narrative, the goal should be to facilitate an environment in which she can choose the memory or sentiment to express, express this with as little reliving of the trauma as possible, and with the group identify any lies she might have believed about herself ("I'm a bad girl"), and the corresponding truth in the Word of God ("I am fearfully and wonderfully made," according to Ps. 139:14).

4. *God's voice is the most powerful transformer of identity.* Each and every time I have taken time during a session to "listen to what Jesus wants to tell us," the Holy Spirit has impressed God's love and value on individuals in a much more tangible, indisputable way than my words could ever induce.

5. *Honor everyone's art, no matter how horrific or simple, powerful or seemingly meaningless.* Create a space that is safe, always honoring, truth-filled, accepting, and challenging. Then when creation of a song, collage, poem, or dance is

facilitated, God—the loving Creator—can be counted on to work in the hearts of those present.

6. *Self-care is critical to the longevity and effectiveness of the caregiver.* After seven months in India, I returned home early, diagnosed with depression, unable to socialize or find joy or even think of India for several months. Through counseling and mentoring I learned that to care for the hurting I had to make my own emotional health a priority. For me, this involved better boundaries and accountability to those who knew me best.

7. *You cannot love a people unless you speak their language.* My first breakthrough with five-year-olds rescued from Asia's largest red-light district was asking them to teach me to count to one hundred in Hindi. We have been like sisters ever since.

FORGE A NEW PATH

Many young artists approach me asking for an organization "like Rescue Arts" to work with in their particular city. When I suggest an after-school program or women's shelter where she can volunteer and propose using the arts for healing, the hopeful young woman usually takes a step back, blinks, and shakes her head. She desires to bring healing through the arts, but she prefers the security of a program to accomplish this.

When I began serving with Project Rescue there was no creative arts component to the ministry, but ministry directors in several cities were open to the possibility. Four different sites gave me permission, with the arts as my primary area of "expertise," to design a project to facilitate healing through the arts. This four- to six-week project looked dramatically different in each of the four cities. As I served under a ministry that was already life-changing and walked with girls in need of healing, I found myself listening, reworking, and shaping a method for local staff to continue after I left.

> There is no shortage of trauma survivors who would benefit from a kind, trustworthy mentor who facilitates expressive, cognitive, and relational development through the arts.

I didn't set out to found a method for bringing healing through the arts. I couldn't have created the method and network that has become Rescue Arts if I had tried in my own strength and wisdom. In a way that only God could orchestrate, because I was present on-the-ground and willing, I began designing creative projects, collaborating with local staff and survivors themselves. I learned responsible ways to facilitate expression and healing through the arts, and learned what did and did not work. I enlisted volunteers in areas of the arts, education, and counseling, and together we solidified a "method" for bringing healing through the arts, and it became known as Rescue Arts. I didn't set out with an end in sight. I served the leaders, women, and children in Project Rescue and God brought something beautiful out of it. I'm the first to admit that Rescue Arts is not the end-all and be-all for using the creative arts for healing. There is much more to be done, creative ones!

There is no shortage of trauma survivors who would benefit from a kind, trustworthy mentor who facilitates expressive, cognitive, and relational development through the arts. There is, however, a shortage of men and women *willing* to make themselves available and to attempt such an endeavor—often without pay. It is not because we have no compassion, but at times we are afraid we will do more damage than good. We are not sure how to start. We aren't sure how to meet "them" and how to organize such a project. My best advice is to find a reputable organization working hands-on with the hurting and begin to serve with them. Soon it will become clear what you can do.

My goal in writing this chapter is that more artists will use the resources available, walk responsibly, set their sights on survivors of trauma who desperately need healing, and forge a new path to bring healing through creativity.

CONCLUSION

In the summer of 2008, I lived in the muggy heat of Kolkata and spent my days with the Project Rescue aftercare home—sixteen girls ages four to sixteen. Each girl had been born in the red-light district and was destined for the slavery of the generations before her. Instead of hiding from customers and roaming the alleys of a human slave market, they lived in a spacious flat overlooking a peaceful pond, attended a good school, and were loved by caring staff. These little ones had grown dramatically in every way since their rescue, but they still carried the shame of secrecy and a stigma society had imposed on them.

A colleague and I led a project involving dance, writing, art, and a final performance for the staff. We led the girls through a process of choosing an animal they related to, telling the story of that animal (we created picture books since many could not write yet), then working together to narrate, choreograph, and perform their stories together. One particularly sweet-faced girl stunned me as she wrote and directed a four- and five-year-old to perform her story.

Shantali wrote of a little rabbit who was abandoned in a bad area and left outside to be beaten and taken advantage of. Her two little actresses wore masks of a bunny and dog. The dog beat the bunny over and over, and the young bunny cried and curled up on the ground. After a time in that bad place the little rabbit was taken in by another animal who truly cared for her. She grew bigger, and then she began to help others. The drama ended with the five-year-old (in a purple bunny mask with a pink nose) hugging the "doggy" (abusive man) and wiping "his" tears. The whole audience of little girls and staff sat in rapt attention, not knowing quite what to say. Through story-telling and an ensemble performance, Shantali and her little comrades had told the ultimate story of Jesus who loves us and gives us new life, giving us the supernatural ability to forgive and help those who have tried to destroy us.

I am consistently amazed at the revelation the Holy Spirit brings to survivors of trauma when they have the opportunity to express, to process, and to bring creativity to life as an ensemble. There is no message or theme I could conjure up more powerful than the raw, guileless creations of those who are walking examples of miraculous wholeness.

SUGGESTED LEARNING EXPERIENCE

Describe a time when creativity—or an area of the arts—provided for a moment of healing in your own life.

Take a moment to ask God whom He might be asking you to serve by facilitating healing through the arts. Jot down the demographic and how you might design a project with this demographic.

Research "best practices" for the demographic you would like to work with, and list a few that you find.

FOR FURTHER STUDY

- Grant, Beth, and Cindy Hudlin, eds. *Hands That Heal: International Curriculum to Train Caregivers of Trafficking Survivors.* N.p.: Faith Alliance Against Slavery and Trafficking, 2007.

- Fujimura, Makoto. *Refractions: A Journey of Faith, Art, and Culture.* Colorado Springs, CO: Navpress, 2009.

- Hughes, Daniel A. *Building the Bonds of Attachment: Awakening Love in Deeply Troubled Children.* 2nd ed. Oxford: Jason Aronson, 2006.

- Kraft, Charles. *Deep Wounds, Deep Healing: Discovering the Vital Link Between Spiritual Warfare and Inner Healing.* Ventura, CA: Gospel Light, 1993.

- Omartian, Stormie. *Lord, I Want to Be Whole: Workbook and Journal.* Nashville, TN: Thomas Nelson Publishers, 2003.

- Linesch, Debra. *Art Therapy with Families in Crisis: Overcoming Resistance Through Nonverbal Expression.* New York: Brunner/Mazel Publishers, 1993.

- Rothschild, B. *Help for the Helper: The Psychophysiology of Compassion Fatigue and Vicarious Trauma.* New York and London: W. W. Norton and Company, 2006.

- Rothschild, B. *The Body Remembers: The Psychophysiology of Trauma and Trauma Treatment.* New York and London: W.W. Norton and Company, 2000.

CHAPTER 10

"HOW CAN WE HELP... BESIDES PRAY?": THE STRATEGY OF INTERCESSION

"Father, may this place which has been known for
great darkness become known as a place where
the Light of Jesus shines most brightly—in salvation,
deliverance, joy, and the transforming work of the
Holy Spirit! May your will be done, may your kingdom
come to Kamatapura for the glory of Your Name!"
PRAYER IN A RED-LIGHT DISTRICT CHURCH, INDIA

A few years ago, I was privileged to participate in a women's retreat during a time of intense intercessory prayer. God's powerful presence was accompanied by a prophetic word describing the extraordinary might of the Lion of Judah. My prayers went immediately to the tens of thousands of women and children within the shadow of Project Rescue-affiliated ministries who desperately need freedom from sexual slavery and new life through Jesus Christ.

Suddenly, God spoke to me that like a lion can cripple its prey by breaking its back and bringing it down, the mighty Lion of Judah is the only One who can break the back of the systems of evil that control sexual exploitation in India and around the world. The most well-intentioned, well-executed human efforts alone cannot disable these destructive systems without the supernatural intervention of the King of Kings who has all power and spiritual authority. It was not enough to pray for individuals to be released from slavery, but we as a ministry team needed to simultaneously pray that the Lion of Judah would break the back of these evil systems that control and perpetuate this injustice, destroying millions of people's lives.

Several months later, we were back in India with ministry colleagues doing intercession in a red-light district outreach center. I felt that I should share the challenge God had shared with me regarding strategic intercession for God to bring down the evil systems that control sexual slavery in that strategic city. Suddenly, staff members who are powerful women of prayer—transformed former madams—began to affirm with tears that God must bring down the crushing systems of darkness they knew all too well. They knew exactly where the power brokers were centered in the city, and of course it was nowhere near the horrific violence and filth of the district but in one of the most affluent areas in the city. As we all began to storm the gates of hell in anointed prayer in a small room in the middle of hell, prostituted women on the street began to quietly knock at the door and enter asking for prayer. God is teaching us how to do battle in Spirit-empowered prayer as we simultaneously act in compassion and do justice.

DEVELOPING INTERCESSORS FOR
COMPASSION AND JUSTICE

There are far too many moments, in attempting to bring hope and healing to exploited women and children, in which I can readily identify with Jesus' disciples. The disciple Matthew recounts the extraordinary experience of Peter, James, and John on the mountain with Jesus when He was transfigured in front of their eyes (Matt. 17:1–8). They were uniquely privileged to witness the Son of God in radiant glory as the Father spoke from heaven in an audible voice saying, "This is my beloved Son in whom I am well pleased. Hear Him!" The impact upon these men was so powerful they fell on their faces on the ground, rising only at the touch and command of Jesus, their Lord.

It is intriguing and somewhat comforting in our humanity to read the account that follows the transfiguration in Matthew 17:14–21. Jesus and His disciples were back with a multitude of people when Jesus was approached by a broken-hearted father on behalf of his epileptic son. In seeking Jesus' help, the father happened to mention that he had already brought his son to Jesus' disciples for healing, *but they could not help the boy* (v. 16). From Matthew's account, it seems that Jesus first rebuked a "faithless and perverse generation" and then went on to rebuke the demon that had afflicted the boy. Immediately, the child was cured and delivered (vv. 17–18).

Privately, the disciples came to Jesus later and asked Him why they had not been able to cast out the demonic power. Privately, I am sympathetic. There have been times when I have stared into the deadened eyes of a young woman who has been brutally raped for money since childhood and seen the reflection of chilling powers of darkness. Like the disciples, I prayed with sincerity, compassion, desperation, and even anger at injustice. But after the prayer was finished, she still walked away in bondage.

"Why couldn't we drive it out?"(v. 19). The disciples' question is neither casual nor unimportant for today's followers of Jesus who are impassioned to be His agents of compassion, healing, and freedom. Perhaps we can just avoid those who are under the influence of demonic power—"That's not my ministry"? Listen closely to Jesus' response. He indicated they had failed because of their lack of faith. Even mustard seed-size faith in Him could move mountains! Then Jesus adds a critical and profound word of instruction for them and for all disciples to come. "This kind [of demonic power] does not go out except by prayer and fasting" (v. 21, NKJV). Simply stated, this is possibly the hardest work in compassion and justice. If we believe what Jesus said, none of our strategies to bring spiritual deliverance from the powers of darkness is sufficient. We must intentionally prioritize—in our days, our schedules, our agendas, our time—to become people of fasting and prayer.

But how do we personally develop into more strategic intercessors in the spiritual battle that is a part of engaging Christ's compassion and justice?

1. *We must acknowledge the reality of the spiritual battle. It's real!* We must recognize that proclaiming Christ's victory on behalf of His integrated mission requires spiritual battle against collective spiritual authorities and powers of evil—even as doing compassion and justice. Some enemies of God's mission are visible, some invisible as referred to by the apostle Paul in Ephesians 6:12: "for our struggle

is not against flesh and blood, but against the rulers,
against the authorities, against the powers of this
dark world and against the spiritual forces of evil in
the heavenly realms." Our mission, God's mission,
is to help men and women bound by these powerful
systems find freedom and deliverance in order to
become strong men and women of God. Spiritual
warfare is unavoidable for victory.

2. *We must do spiritual warfare in intercession against*
evil systems while extending Christ's unconditional
love to individuals enslaved in the evil system.
Thankfully for the little four-year-old girl in the
red-light district church who took my breath
away (see chapter 6), the director of Bombay Teen
Challenge, K. K. Devaraj, understands both her
personal need for Jesus and the need to proclaim
Christ's authority over evil systems for the sake
of every person enslaved in them. In this biblical
integration of intercession against evil structures
with Christ's personal that-none-should-perish
mission, Devaraj and his ministry team do not
practice selective compassion. They reach out boldly
in love, like Jesus, to the whole community caught
in Satan's destructive schemes—to madams, pimps,
corrupt policemen, local government officials,
"customers," and to the women and children they
exploit. The impact of this approach is evident as the
strongest workers in the red-light district ministry
today are former madams and their children who
were set free—body, mind, and spirit—years ago.

A pimp has been heard to turn brothel "customers" temporarily away because the BTC outreach team was conducting a Bible study there for women hungry for God. Devaraj dares to proclaim Christ's compassion and power where Satan rules, and as a result, men, women, and children are miraculously finding Jesus there.

3. *We must learn to pray Spirit-infused, Spirit-inspired prayers of proclamation.* God is leading His people to pray powerful prayers of faith, claiming Christ's victory over religious, economic, and political systems that perpetuate injustice. Systems can become tools of Satan to destroy not only individuals, but communities and generations of people around the world. A pastor in Asia known as a man of prayer leads his congregation in daily, weekly, monthly, and annual cycles of fervent Pentecostal intercession. During one of the monthly all-night prayer meetings with thousands of believers, he began to publicly pray a prophetic prayer worthy of the Old Testament prophets. The pastor was not pleading with God. He was not being presumptuous, but rather walking in great humility. But because of his life of daily fervent prayer and spending time in God's presence, he proclaimed Christ's authority through prayer as he discerned in the Spirit God's destiny for his city, nation, and continent. "Father, may the pagan idols in this nation be brought down and melt into the seas! May the cross of Christ be proclaimed from north to

south, from east to west! May this pagan continent
become a Christian continent! "This bold prayer
of proclamation was fitting for the greatness of our
omnipotent God and reminiscent of the prophetic
ministry God spoke over Jeremiah. "I have put my
words in your mouth. See, today I appoint you over
nations and kingdoms to uproot and tear down, to
destroy and overthrow, to build and to plant"
(Jer. 1:9–10). The community of faith in the city has
grown over 10 percent, and the church is casting
a great shadow for Christ's kingdom across the
continent. The God who does not change still uses
men and women in the same way to pray prayers of
prophetic proclamation that can change their cities,
nations, and even our twenty-first-century world.

4. *We must humbly acknowledge our need to grow in
intercessory spiritual warfare.* We have much to learn.
Over time, men and women of God have walked
in spiritual authority as they heard God's voice and
responded in intercession and proclamation for
cities and nations, and against systems of injustice.
Some have been theologically sound; some have
not. In some cases, we may observe in the same
minister aspects of spiritual warfare on the corporate
level that are sound and other areas of practice we
question. But we must be careful not to throw the
proverbial baby out with the bath water. Instead,
there are uncomfortable questions we must ask
ourselves. Our theology and doctrine may be
sound—but what spiritual impact are we personally

and corporately making on the tsunami of evil sweeping our cities and nation? Is the darkness of Satan being challenged in our cities because we are there engaging prophetically in the power of the Spirit? Or are we guilty of being doctrinally pure and spiritually powerless? Are we more experienced in judging how others are doing spiritual warfare than we are at doing spiritual warfare ourselves? Like the disciples who came back to Jesus, having dismally failed in dealing with demonic power (at least they tried!), we also have room for growth.

May God grant His people in all parts of His church the humility to learn from one another across denominations and affiliations. If our ears and hearts are open, God can teach us valuable lessons on spiritual warfare through other men and women of God, sometimes in unexpected places.

SAVING CHILDREN, STORMING HELL

Ruth and her husband, Thomas, (not their real names) confront systems of evil every day. Six years ago, God called them to minister in a red-light district of an extremely dark Asian city. God's anointing was upon them, and the ministry among prostituted women and their children began to grow quickly. Within five years, over one-hundred children of women in sex slavery were released into safe homes where they received medical help, education, counseling, and Jesus.

Ruth and Thomas earned the confidence of many in the community who came to receive prayer and medical help. A Sunday service was begun in the community for prostituted women to begin their spiritual journeys to freedom. These are miracles in any city, but especially in a city of over one million people, which has a long-documented history of paganism and violent opposition to any Christian influence. Every level of society where power is held is infiltrated by the forces of evil. Every step of faith taken to challenge the darkness is met with open and powerful opposition.

Ruth is an irrepressible, courageous woman of intercession. She has repeatedly received court summons instigated by those who have a stake in seeing rescued young girls sent back into "the business." The healthier and happier the little girls become in their new lives in Christ, the greater their street value to pimps, madams, "fathers," corrupt policemen, and even desperate enslaved mothers. Unfortunately, the red-light district is controlled by powerful political, religious, and economic systems collaborating in their unjust cause.

On one occasion, Ruth was summoned to court because the director of the Woman and Child Welfare Society was attempting to close the ministry by bringing charges of child abuse. Ruth's family and colleagues covered her in prayer as she appeared in court to respond to this powerful director. When called to testify, Ruth had such a strong sense of God's presence with her that she challenged the official, who had never actually visited the ministry homes, to come and see them before pressing her case. With the public invitation and revelation that the woman had never actually seen the ministry she was accusing, she accepted Ruth's invitation. This woman of influence visited the ministry sites, saw the work, dropped the case, and ultimately became an advocate for the Christian ministry in an unjust system.

But the battle does not end. Until Jesus establishes His kingdom on earth, the spiritual attacks are constant and unrelenting through systems of injustice. On another occasion, Ruth and Thomas worked tirelessly to persuade a prostituted woman to release her beautiful seven-year-old daughter from the brothel into the aftercare ministry home for children. Their goal is to get little girls out of harm's way as a preventive measure, so they will not be sexually exploited and forced into sex slavery by eleven and twelve years of age. After much prayer and effort, the mother released her daughter into the couple's care where she could receive Christ's healing love, education, and safety. The beautiful little girl flourished. Tragically, under threats of violence from those who control the injustice of which the mother was herself a victim, she returned to Ruth and Thomas and insisted that her daughter be released to her to return to the red-light district. In spite of tearful appeals, the mother took her daughter back into the world of darkness—where the child was gang-raped by men and died an unimaginably horrible death. There are no words to adequately express the horror and carnage of Satan's evil systems. The only consolation is that this precious child went to be with the Jesus she had learned to love and has a safe home forever with Him. She can never be exploited again.

Ruth and Thomas and the staff grieved the tragic death of the little girl they'd come to love. Yet they made an unnatural but Christ-like choice to begin to minister His compassion to the grief-stricken mother. She was mentally and emotionally tormented by her daughter's death and her own part in it. They offered her Christ's unconditional love and forgiveness, knowing that Christ's freedom, forgiveness, redemption, and new life are available even for her. As the apostle Peter proclaimed, "The Lord is not slow in keeping his promise, as some understand slowness. Instead he is patient with you, not wanting anyone to perish, but everyone to come to repentance" (2 Pet. 3:9).

Seven years later, this formerly devastated woman has received God's forgiveness and continues her healing journey with Jesus in a community of faith. A woman who was part of a system perpetuating slavery in her own daughter's life is now a valuable staff member in a ministry helping other rescued children in their journey to healing. She is free, and she has a new identity in Christ! And on the most difficult days, she finds hope in knowing she will be with Jesus and her daughter in heaven one day.

> When compassion and justice are life-changing long-term, someone is paying the price to wage spiritual battle against darkness through Spirit-empowered prayer.

And when people ask how they can help—besides pray? Every day, every step, every victory in Ruth and Thomas' story is challenged by systems of evil and won through evil-defeating spiritual warfare. When compassion and justice are life-changing long-term, someone is paying the price to wage spiritual battle against darkness through Spirit-empowered prayer.

PROCLAIMING CHRIST'S VICTORY AND KINGDOM OVER UNJUST SOCIAL SYSTEMS

Here are some strategic prayer points for spiritual warfare when God's people face systemic injustice in fulfilling the Great Commission:

- For God-given favor and prerequisite relationships
  with government officials, agency leaders, local
  people of authority, pimps, madams—anyone who
  controls systems of injustice on local, regional, and
  national levels.

- For the salvation of men and women in high places
  who are perpetuating systems of injustice.

- For the bringing down of political, economic, legal,
  and physical strongholds that control thousands in
  our cities whom Christ came to set free.

- For supernatural protection over believers called to
  bring Jesus to those whose lives are controlled by
  organized crime and evil systems.

- For godly leaders to be Spirit-led, discerning,
  strategic, and anointed to proclaim Christ's victory
  over specific bastions of darkness in their cities.

- For a growing army of courageous men and women
  of God who will be led of the Spirit in spiritual
  warfare and unflinchingly obedient to proclaim
  Christ's victory!

CONCLUSION: BEYOND WEEPING TO WARRING TO TRIUMPH

There is no more powerful image of intercession in the face of Satan's evil strategies against God's redemptive mission than that of Jesus agonizing in Gethsemane (Luke 22:39–46). But the battle was not complete in the garden of intercession. Calvary had to follow, where the epic battle against all Satan's schemes and systems were defeated on a criminal's cross. And in God's mysterious ways, an empty tomb will forever represent Jesus' resurrection life and victory over sin, Satan, and death. Every evil system and structure was defeated at Calvary along with the arch-enemy who devised them.

Tragically, the kingdom of darkness in our cities, nation, and world is certain—if God's people avoid, shirk, ignore, or timidly refuse to engage in spiritual battle against Satan's systemic schemes. But victory for the kingdom of God in our cities is divinely ordained—if God's people discern His strategic purposes, intercede against systems of injustice, and boldly proclaim Christ's victory over evil. The Lord of the battle prophesied, "On this rock I will build my church, and the gates [or schemes] of Hades [hell] will not overcome it" (Matt. 16:18). May His kingdom come! We have a greater awareness that as the apostle Paul attested, "our struggle is not against flesh and blood but against the rulers, against the authorities, against the powers of this dark world and against the spiritual forces of evil in the heavenly realms" (Eph. 6:12). Acts of courageous compassion and justice require equally courageous prayers!

SUGGESTED LEARNING EXPERIENCE

The pastoral leadership of First Assembly of God, Bangalore, India, developed a strategic prayer calendar for their congregation, which is shared here as a tool. It's a practical example of integrating spiritual warfare with God's Word, compassion, and justice in a specific city and local context. (Note that only three out of four weeks have been included here as the third week was focused on prayer for individuals and is not appropriate to share.)

First Assembly of God Church, Bangalore, India Chain of Prayer Schedule (Nov – Dec 2013)

WEEK ONE

However, as it is written: "What no eye has seen, what no ear has heard, and what no human mind has conceived"—the things God has prepared for those who love him. (1 Corinthians 2:9)

MONDAY **Zechariah 7:9–10**

Pray that we as a church will truly understand the heart of God in the matter of justice in our land. Pray that we will strive for understanding to enforce justice in all areas of our lives and continue to plead the cause of justice.

TUESDAY **Romans 12:15–21**

Pray that we will continue to seek and receive knowledge from the Lord on our approach in every situation. Pray that our responses will be born out of love. Pray that we will continue in the purity of heart that will delight God.

WEDNESDAY   **Matthew 7:12**

Pray that as our love for the Lord consumes us, we will continue to abide in His Word and follow His commandments. Pray that God will use us to continue to heal, deliver, and set captives free.

THURSDAY   **1 John 3:17–18**

Pray that God will continue to stir us to be channels of blessing to others. Pray that His love for us will spur us on to greater love for Him that will spill over. Pray that we will continue to be known by love.

FRIDAY   **Isaiah 58:6–11**

Pray that our prayers and petitions will continue to be aligned with the will of God. Pray that they will be unselfish and strike a chord in the Father's heart. Pray for knowledge to place right petitions before Him.

SATURDAY   **James 1:27**

Pray that we will continue to cherish purity and hate defiling the things of God. Pray that even as we live in the world, we will remain separated from the ways of the world. Pray that we will bring joy to the Father in all we do.

SUNDAY   **Amos 5:24**

Pray that we will continue to seek the ways of the Lord, to walk in justice and righteousness that brings peace to the land. Pray that the Spirit of God will be with us in might and power in all that we do, for His glory.

WEEK TWO

Pray that we as a church will stand strong, totally dependent on the Lord for His mission forward and will fulfill the work that God has assigned to us a church. Pray for the anti-human trafficking network in Bangalore.

MONDAY

United Theological College, Women's Studies Dept.
Pray for the department that strives to create awareness of injustice and oppression in society. Pray that their work will bring the change in society that is desired by God. Pray for God's direction and protection for those in authority.

TUESDAY

Project Rescue
Pray for the hand of God to be with them in their work of prevention and intervention in cases of human trafficking and restoration of individuals rescued. Pray for the directors and the workers for God's protection and direction.

WEDNESDAY

Global Concerns India
Pray for continued resources for organization to respond to the calls of the oppressed. Pray for God's protection and wisdom for the directors and the workers on the field. Pray that they will be successful in spreading awareness.

THURSDAY

International Justice Mission
Pray for favor of God and increased influence with the government authorities. Pray for God's wisdom for the lawyers who seek justice for the

oppressed. Pray for all the directors and workers for God's special protection and direction.

FRIDAY   **Justice and Care**

Pray for God's discernment and knowledge for all those who work with law enforcement agencies in the matter of rescued children and young adults from slavery. Pray that God will favor their work and keep them on the right path.

SATURDAY   **Asha Forum**

Pray for God's protection over the people who are part of this forum. Pray for greater impact of their work among the Christians of the nation. Pray that God will use them to bring more children into His marvelous light.

SUNDAY   **Women of Destiny, Bangalore Prayer Meeting**

Pray for God's protection over the leaders of this movement. Pray for greater faith to break the yoke of the enemy over the weak and oppressed. Pray for greater influence of prayer in all areas of the society at large.

WEEK THREE

Pray that in the stirring of His wrath over this sin against Him, He will look upon everyone with mercy, upon the perpetrators and the victims to establish His peace and justice over the nation. Pray against illegal activities related to human trafficking.

MONDAY

Kidnapping

Pray that God will protect innocent, potential victims most likely to be targeted for inducting into the human trafficking network. Pray that God would confound all tactics of the Enemy. Pray for greater awareness among children of the dangers of kidnapping.

TUESDAY

Pornography

Pray against the networks spanning nations that make and distribute pornography. Pray that God will expose the roots of such networks. Pray that coaches and teachers will operate in the fear of God and desist from working for the networks. Pray for the safety of children.

WEDNESDAY

Substance Abuse

Pray against the network that produces, processes, markets, and distributes drugs. Pray that God will rise against these ventures with wrath and anger. Pray that youth and children will recognize and avoid traps that will lure them into substance abuse.

THURSDAY

Murder

Pray that innocent lives will not be snuffed out by evil intentions of the human traffickers. Pray that God will continue to use His people to come against this evil, protect lives, and save souls. Pray that He will continue to set captives free in supernatural ways.

FRIDAY

Pedophilia

Pray against this evil thing that preys upon the bodies of children. Pray that God will hear the cry of children forced into unnatural acts that God never intended. Pray that He will rise up and rescue them, heal them, make them new, and lead them gently into His way.

SATURDAY

Organ Trade

Pray against this oppressive trade where innocent people are robbed of their organs for gain. Pray that God will reveal consequences that man will be afraid to engage in this trade. Pray for greater awareness among villagers of this danger, that they be wary of strangers.

SUNDAY

Extortion

Pray against those who make a parasitic living by extorting money from others. Pray that all plans and strategies to entangle more people into this way of life will be nullified. Pray for shame to overcome the hearts of those who indulge in this trade.

QUESTIONS TO EXPLORE:

1. What stands out to you as you first read the prayer calendar? Why?

2. The prayer calendar focuses on the specific injustice of human trafficking and its related evils because this has become a disturbingly common horror in that city and nation. What would be the most pressing

injustice(s) in your community that God is placing
on your heart individually, as a small group,
or congregation?

3. Prayerfully (yes, prayerfully!) develop a strategic
prayer calendar with your small group or leadership
team that you can use to mobilize people to Spirit-
empowered intercession for justice and against the
spiritual powers and systems of injustice. Research
and include appropriate Scripture to guide the prayer
initiative, both individual and community focuses,
and prayer for other local faith-based organizations
who share the same God-given mission.

FOR FURTHER STUDY

- Murray, Andrew. *The Ministry of Intercessory Prayer:
  A Classic Devotional Edited for Today's Reader.*
  Minneapolis, MN: Bethany House, 2003.

- Nouwen, Henri J. *The Only Necessary Thing: Living a
  Prayerful Life.* New York: The Crossroad Publishing
  Company, 2008.

- Sheets, Dutch. *Authority in Prayer: Praying with
  Power and Purpose.* Minneapolis, MN: Bethany
  House, 2006.

CHAPTER 11

THE MAFIA GETS IT. WHY DON'T WE?: THE UNDERTAPPED POWER OF COLLABORATION

"I can do it—all by myself!"
AMERICAN TODDLERS' FAVORITE STATEMENT

Alone we can do so little; together we can do so much.
HELEN KELLER

There are different kinds of gifts, but the
same Spirit distributes them.
There are different kinds of service, but the same Lord.
There are different kinds of working, but in all of them
and in everyone it is the same God at work.
Now you are the body of Christ, and
each one of you is a part of it.
1 CORINTHIANS 12:4-6, 27

My husband, David, and I were in an Iranian church in London where he was speaking. He was describing the injustice of sex trafficking around the world and how it works. Like many times before, David began to list the different national and international organized crime syndicates that have developed formidable global networks for selling sex. They are feared and disturbingly effective at perpetrating this particular evil, and go virtually unchallenged in far too many nations of the world.

Suddenly, it struck me. If organized crime can work together for their shared purposes of greed, exploitation, and injustice, why in the world can't good people—God's people—work together for the sake of accomplishing His purposes of freedom, healing, and justice?[72]

NO, WE CANNOT DO IT ALONE!

Hopefully by now, as you have read this book, the complexity of challenging injustice and helping survivors find freedom and healing has become more and more apparent. The intent is not to discourage a bold, obedient compassion in response to God's love and mission for victims. The opposite is true. But one of the primary passions behind writing this book has been the growing certainty that we cannot do it alone!

Unfortunately, too many of us think we can. Monthly if not weekly, my husband, our office staff, and I are contacted by well-meaning, passionate young people who have a burden for trafficked women and children. They are wonderfully sincere and generous, and their burden is as genuine as their love for God. However,

---

72 "While crime groups sometimes compete violently with each other for control over territory and franchise, at other times they cooperate when such cooperation is seen as mutually beneficial to all parties." From Marci Cottingham, Thomas Nowak, Kay Snyder, and Melissa Swauger in "Sociological Perspective: Underlying Causes," chapter 3 in *Human Trafficking: Interdisciplinary Perspectives* by Mary Burke (New York: Routledge, 2013) 61. Also refer to www.faastinternational.org.

thanks to our American sacrilization of rugged individualism, we tend to assume if we have a burden for something, God is telling us to start something. So often, the first steps we hear that people have taken to follow up on their passion for trafficked women and children look something like this:

1. Pray about it.
2. Tell their friends (or parents) what they are going to do.
3. Pick a name for the initiative.
4. Develop a logo.
5. Develop a website.
6. Raise money.
7. Become a voice/advocate.

Then our family and friends applaud our passion and individual initiative, but the present and long-term impact is minimized because it is based on one individual's vision, initiative, and capacity. After years of painful lessons learned on this journey of compassion ministry, we would modify the steps to look something like this:

1. Pray about it.
2. Talk to family, friends, and respected mentors about the need and your burden for it. Seek their advice and listen.
3. Pray together about the need.

4. Do some homework to find out who is already doing something with prostituted women and/or sexually abused children in your community or city (homeless shelters, food kitchens in areas of prostitution or drugs, social services, churches programs to the poor, etc.). Most likely someone is already doing something related to this injustice. Find out who and what.

5. Bring information back to respected mentors and pray together about what God might have you all do as a group or church to meet a part of the need.

6. Volunteer part-time with one of the local initiatives. This will give you opportunity to interact with exploited women and children. Out of those basic experiences, God can begin to clarify the passion He has placed on your heart.

7. But your burden is for this kind of work overseas? Start in your home culture first. It's very hard to do in another country, in a different language and culture, what we have never done in our own culture. If God is directing us to work with the sexually exploited or prostituted women and children, being around them as a volunteer in our own community and culture will only confirm His heart for them in us, even though it may be difficult. Organize a small group of those who are committed to this need. Share the information you've all gleaned about local needs together and seek God's direction about practical next steps.

8. Invite professionals who work with anti-trafficking and victims services to share with your small group or church (i.e., law enforcement, social services, the director of an NGO working with this need). Ask them what you could do as a church or group to help them. They will respect your compassion and respect even more your sincere inquiry as to how you can help rather than running ahead, oblivious of their efforts and expertise.

You can initiate these eight steps without any appreciable need for funding, forming an NGO, or developing a website. *First things first!* The foundation is laid for anything life-changing and lasting through group prayer, building relationships in the local community, asking good questions, listening to informed answers, and planning for action together—not alone. And the potential impact is multiplied now and into the future because of collaboration.

The old African proverb couldn't be more right as it relates to building ministries to victims of injustice. "If you want to go fast, go alone. If you want to go far, go together."

> The old African proverb couldn't be more right as it relates to building ministries to victims of injustice. "If you want to go fast, go alone. If you want to go far, go together.

A MODEL FOR COLLABORATION IN COMPASSION AND JUSTICE

It was in the "aha" moment in the Iranian church in London that I first tried to visualize the complexity of doing genuinely life-changing compassion and justice collaboratively as followers of Jesus. The following model resulted and has been adapted in many forms. It demonstrates the multi-faceted nature of holistic compassion ministry and why partnering with other individuals, organizations, churches, and denominations is critical for greater effectiveness in the battle for justice locally and globally.

COLLABORATION FOR LIFE-CHANGING COMPASSION

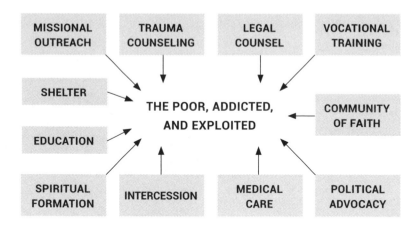

No one ministry or organization is the answer. Jesus is. Doing His justice, freedom, healing, and deliverance requires collaboration!

THE GREATEST CHALLENGE FOR FAITH-BASED INITIATIVES IN FIGHTING INJUSTICE

In *Courageous Compassion* I have attempted to address some of the most pertinent challenges that face those who obey God's call to act on behalf of victims of injustice: fear, our own expectations, the community of darkness, the power of organized crime, and the spiritual forces of darkness. However, we have come to the conclusion that the one challenge most difficult to address and potentially most crippling to God's powerful promises at work is the lack of desire, willingness, and ability of good people called of God to this mission to actually work together. It's not a pretty picture. The twenty-first-century battleground between the forces of justice and injustice in our world is strewn with the casualties of broken relationships, broken partnerships, and wounded, God-called warriors.

There are some good qualities that come out of our individualistic worldview when it comes to doing God's justice and compassion: initiative, individual courage, the ability to hear God's voice and act on it even when it's not popular or easy, and the willingness to set goals and accomplish them. But there are corollary qualities that come along with our cultural individualism that are counterproductive to doing justice and compassion effectively, and even unbiblical. A Western model for success applauds leaders who are independent, self-sufficient, self-promoting, and highly competitive. But these qualities can wreak havoc in the attempts of people of faith to fight injustice and bring healing compassion to our world together. Our cultural strengths can become our weaknesses both spiritually and practically. We are indeed one in the body of Christ in spirit; yet in far too many cases, we have become so adept at fighting and crippling one another in the battle against evil and injustice, that the Evil One has little to fear.

A great missionary mentor and leader of my husband's and mine was Dr. Charles Greenaway. He promised us on many occasions, "I'll do everything I can to help you. But if I can't help you, at least I won't hurt you!" In the twenty-first-century battle against injustice, it would be battle-changing if we made that commitment to one another as well.

WHY CAN'T FAITH-BASED COMPASSIONATE ORGANIZATIONS WORK TOGETHER?

The Western (and increasingly, global) value on competition that we embrace so unquestioningly has practical implications when we attempt to collaborate for the sake of the broken and enslaved in our world. In 2006, the steering committee of the Faith Alliance Against Slavery and Trafficking (FAAST)[73] determined that our greatest need internationally among our member organizations was for a developed curriculum to train caregivers for trafficking survivors. It would include over forty practitioners and writers from many different faith communities. Then, as we took our proposal to our respective organizational leaders, the first kinds of questions asked were:

1. Who will own the final product?
2. Who will hold the copyright?
3. Where will the profits go?

---

73 See www.faastinternational.org.

In your mind, you may be thinking, "Of course those are the natural questions. What is your point?" My husband and I quietly countered, "This project is about the kingdom. It will belong to all of us. It's not about any one of our member organizations. It's bigger than Project Rescue. This is about working together across denominations and faith organizations globally for the

> When we get close enough to know each other, we learn to love, understand, and value one another and discover that many of our stereotypes are unfair and ungrounded

sake of helping victims of sexual slavery find freedom and get the healing care they desperately need.[74] We are bringing our strengths together for the sake of the mission."

Naïve? Perhaps, but isn't much Jesus calls us to do and how He calls us to do it naïve through the eyes of secular culture? Yes, collaborating across organizations and denominations is difficult. We are all set in our organizational ways. But it is possible—when we prioritize the fulfillment of God's great mission of justice over our personal and organizational preferences. We don't need to collaborate together in all areas in order to collaborate together in some.

But wait a minute—what about faith-based communities that don't share our theology? Can we work together to do justice if we don't share the same doctrine on the Holy Spirit? We pray differently! Hmmm. Could we possibly become so engaged taking Jesus to those in great darkness in our city (and fighting the inevitable accompanying spiritual battles) that we thank God for

---

74 See *Hands that Heal*, 2007.

our brothers and sisters in Christ in the trenches of the battleground with us? When we get close enough to know each other, we learn to love, understand, and value one another and discover that many of our stereotypes are unfair and ungrounded. When we begin to love and respect one another in Christ's love across the community of faith, our desire grows to protect one another across ministries as we work together for the greater purpose of making Christ known and bringing freedom to the most vulnerable in our world. When we face Isaiah 59 violence and darkness, we realize how blessed we are to work together with those who love and trust in Jesus.

Then, there is the "elephant in the room" when it comes to encouraging organizations, nonprofits, and denominational initiatives to work together: fund-raising. All organizations must raise sufficient funding to support their work of compassion and justice. Ironically, faith-based entities that would be well-served and strengthened by working together can easily view themselves as competing with each other for what is perceived to be the same limited pool of charitable donations. Suddenly, good, faith-based organizations doing the same thing for the same Lord find themselves competing against each other, promoting against each other, and in some cases, perhaps unwittingly, undermining each other—all in the name of Jesus! Something is wrong with this picture. It's time we were honest and addressed the "elephant."

A first step in doing this is to recognize we have a problem in letting finances drive our actions and attitudes toward brothers and sisters in Christ focused on the same kinds of work. Personal and corporate repentance is in order for actions or attitudes that are uncomfortably inconsistent with the humility and servant heart of Christ. Secondly, for the sake of our Father's name and mission, let's humbly clear up misunderstandings as they inevitably come in the spirit of Hebrews 12:14: "Make every effort to live in peace with everyone and to be holy. . . ." Third, the God who calls us to His mission is ultimately our provider. He has more than enough resources in His world to supply our needs without undermining other good organizations, churches, and brothers and sisters in His church. If God doesn't, then how can we in good conscience encourage the poor and needy to trust Him with their needs?

One of the most inspiring collaborations focused on victims of sexual exploitation that we have encountered is the Mukti Network in India. Pastor G. Satyanandan has helped mobilize chapters of Mukti Network in several Indian cities to bring together the many faith-based organizations working in areas of prostitution in those cities. In monthly network meetings, each organization's personnel provide updates on their outreach, share pertinent information, and most importantly, pray together for one another in the complex personal and organizational challenges each person faces. The Mukti Network meetings have become a source of needed friendships ("We are not alone in this work!"); shared information about who is doing what; training; and intercession essential to this formidable spiritual battle against evil. In between meetings, organizational leaders refer people to each other's organizations when new personnel inquire or when needs arise in the red-light district. Now that they know each other, members recognize who is doing what well, and can refer people, resources, and needs accordingly. Some of the organizations represented are large, well-funded, and globally powerful. Some are small, struggling, and local. But in the Mukti Network, they come together as brothers and sisters in Christ who need God's help and each other's encouragement. May God enable His people to build thousands of such empowering collaborative networks across our cities and nations for His glory and work.

THE ROLE OF FORGIVENESS

All of us who have served in any way to fulfill God's mission on this earth have experienced hurt and betrayal in the process of trying to work together with other believers. It comes with the territory because we work with people and people are human—just like us.

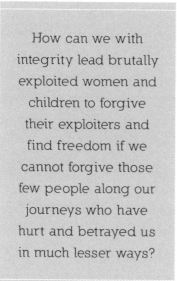

How can we with integrity lead brutally exploited women and children to forgive their exploiters and find freedom if we cannot forgive those few people along our journeys who have hurt and betrayed us in much lesser ways?

But the process of collaboration changes more than the quantity and quality of our compassionate work. Collaboration over time changes us, God's children.

Those who work closely with victims of sexual abuse or exploitation know the critical importance of forgiveness to the healing process. With all the intervention involved in the healing process, a certain level of emotional, psychological, and spiritual healing in survivors requires them to come to a place where they can choose to forgive their abusers. Humanly speaking, given the atrocities committed against millions of them, forgiveness seems impossible.

But something supernatural occurs when those who have begun to receive God's grace dare extend it to those who have hurt them—something liberating, something healing, something empowering—something like Jesus. This does not mean survivors put themselves back in harm's way to be exploited again. But it's transformational when they realize that because of Jesus' love and grace in their lives, they can choose not only to receive grace and forgiveness; they can choose to extend it. And in doing so, some of the controlling power their abusers and the Enemy of their souls have had over them is spiritually broken.

My question to you, my readers, and to myself and all who share a passion to bring freedom and justice to those in slavery is this: How can we with integrity lead brutally exploited women and children to forgive their exploiters and find freedom if we cannot forgive those few people along our journeys who have hurt and betrayed us in much lesser ways? In the words of Jesus, who taught us to pray:

> And forgive us our debts as we also have forgiven our debtors.... For if you forgive other people when they sin against you, your heavenly Father will also forgive you. But if you do not forgive others their sins, your Father will not forgive your sins (Matt. 6:12, 14–15).

And in the apostle Paul's admonition to us:

> Be kind and compassionate to one another, forgiving each other, just as in Christ God forgave you (Eph. 4:32).

In order to counsel victims of injustice to forgive their exploiters with integrity, we too must be willing to live a life of forgiveness toward those who have hurt us. Day-to-day collaboration with others on this compassionate journey provides opportunity to experience and model God's grace for victims of injustice in practical, life-changing ways.

Global organized crime chooses to set aside differences to accomplish a shared destructive mission. It's time God's people do the same to accomplish His loving, liberating, healing, and redemptive one!

CONCLUSION

Extending Christ's courageous compassion and justice in a formidably unjust world requires an unprecedented level of collaboration in the local and global community of faith. It is not only victims of injustice and exploitation who need God's transforming love. We, the community of faith-based responders to injustice, need His transforming love as well.

Heavenly Father,
In a world of self-promotion, may we your sons and daughters become known for
commending the worthy work of others.
In a world of stored grievances, may we become known for our generous grace.
In a world dominated by self-interest, may we be known for preferring others above ourselves.
In a world of competitiveness, may we be known for our Christ-compelled love.
In the powerful name of Jesus, our Lord.
Amen

Then make my joy complete by being like-minded, having the same love, being one in spirit and of one mind (Phil. 2:2).

SUGGESTED LEARNING ACTIVITY

In your small group or class, discuss the following questions:

1. How do you view competitiveness? While it's at the heart of traditional Northern European and American cultures, how does it fit with the life of Christ and New Testament teaching for His followers? What place does it have in doing justice?

2. Revisit the diagram, "Collaboration for Life-Changing Compassion." Where do you see the strengths and potential of your local church, organization, or of yourself? Identify areas of needed skills and ministries that could be filled through collaboration. With whom in your city could you partner in justice and compassion? Prayerfully consider possible next steps toward that goal.

3. Collaboration necessary to do God's mission as God intends is never easy. Look at two to three examples of collaboration by the disciples in the New Testament. Where were their tensions, and how did they resolve them? What practical insights can you glean for your compassion ministry setting?

4. Discuss some of the possible reasons why you, your small group, or church (organization) have not collaborated more. Are they cultural, personal, organizational, promotional, or spiritual? Prayerfully consider how to collaborate more in doing God's compassion and justice more effectively in your

city. Pray over the challenges and ask for wisdom in knowing how a stronger army fulfilling God's mission across your city and state could be developed in a way that better represents God and the biblical community of faith.

FOR FURTHER STUDY

- Hamalainen, Arto, and Grant McClung. *Together in One Mission: Pentecostal Cooperation in World Evangelization.* Cleveland, TN: Pathway Press, 2012.

- Volf, Miroslav. *Free of Charge: Giving and Forgiving in a Culture Stripped of Grace.* Grand Rapids, MI: Zondervan, 2005.

CHAPTER 12

SUPERNATURAL POWER FOR A SUPERNATURAL COMPASSION

I am going to send you what my Father has promised; but stay in
the city until you have been clothed with power from on high.

LUKE 24:49

Oh, spread the tidings 'round, wherever man is found,
Wherever human hearts and human woes abound;
Let every Christian tongue proclaim the joyful sound:
The Comforter has come!
The Comforter has come, the Comforter has come!
The Holy Ghost from Heav'n, the Father's promise giv'n;
Oh, spread the tidings 'round, wherever man is found—
The Comforter has come!
Lo, the great King of kings, with healing in His wings,
To every captive soul a full deliv'rance brings;
And through the vacant cells the song of triumph rings;
The Comforter has come!

SONG BY FRANK BOTTOME, 1890

Several years ago, we were in Mumbai ministering with our
colleague K. K. Devaraj. One afternoon, he suggested we go

to a specific brothel to pray for a woman there who was seriously ill and requesting prayer. I was thankful for the open heart of a woman who desperately needed God's loving touch and for Devaraj's open door to minister to her. At that time, we had a particularly gifted young woman working with us who was passionate about the trafficking issue and helping women find freedom. She represents some of the best of young women called of God to missions in the twenty-first century. Competent, creative, courageous, and confident, this young colleague jumped at the opportunity to go into the district with us to pray that day.

> Every time we have had the opportunity to take the compassionate, life-changing Jesus into darkness, it challenges every bit of faith, courage, and commitment we can muster.

Then, we got out of the car and stepped off the main street in Mumbai into the first lane of the red-light district. Suddenly, with five steps, you leave a world of relative safety where you have some semblance of control and protection into a world of unimaginably normalized exploitation, demonism, and palpable evil. As a woman, perhaps especially as a foreign woman, one is made immediately aware by the atmosphere and men's merciless, all-too-close, penetrating stares that you're no longer in your world; you're in theirs. You're in the wrong place—in the Enemy's territory—and anything can happen.

But just as suddenly, something else had changed. The confident young woman beside me who had been ready to take on the global injustice of trafficking just hours before was reaching quietly and uncertainly for my arm. "Can I hold on to you?" she whispered. Without a word, we locked arms and headed into the streets of hell.

MORE THAN AN OPTION

I understood. Every time we have had the opportunity to take the compassionate, life-changing Jesus into darkness, it challenges every bit of faith, courage, and commitment we can muster. It never gets easy to face the power of evil up close. Why? Because the "powers of darkness" are not metaphors. They are real—and they are bigger, greater, and more powerful than we are. Humanly speaking, we're no match. And on some real estate in some cities, the evil is dauntingly aggressive. You're on one street, and you think you can handle it. Then, you cross the line into the devil's unchallenged territory, and your good sense intrudes, *"What was I thinking?"* Fear can be gripping.

That's why the words of the prophet Zechariah cannot be ignored: "'Not by might, nor by power, but by My Spirit,' says the LORD Almighty" (Zech. 4:6). Doing the work of God's kingdom—even compassion work—cannot be accomplished God's way in our human might or power. It's impossible to do compassion and justice with transformational results without being empowered by the Spirit of the Lord. God is doing something great and worth celebrating in the hearts of His people globally. Many of Jesus' followers across evangelical, Pentecostal, and Charismatic communities in the twenty-first century are embracing His mandate for ministry in Luke 4:18: preaching the gospel to the poor, healing the broken-hearted, proclaiming liberty to captives, recovery of sight to the blind, and setting at liberty the oppressed. For some, this is a renewed commitment; for others, it's a new, theological-box-stretching journey. But in all cases, it's critical that we do not weaken our mission by missing Jesus' stated empowerment for accomplishing these tasks. "The Spirit of the Lord is upon me. Because He has anointed Me."

In the New Testament, God indicates His intended empowerment for life-changing ministry that was revealed in Jesus was for His followers as well. Before the Day of Pentecost, Peter was the verbal, sword-swinging, but pitifully powerless disciple (John 18:17)—a dangerous combination! But days later, when Peter received the promised infilling of the Holy Spirit, he became a powerful and articulate man of God through whom thousands were saved (Acts 2:41).

If the supernatural empowerment of the Holy Spirit were not available to Jesus' followers today, then the mission God has called us to do is impossible. Dubious? Go spend some time on the street in the most dangerous parts of your city trying to engage those who are mentally, emotionally, physically, and spiritually in bondage to demonic power. Have you ever tried talking people out of bondage?

> The empowerment of the Holy Spirit is not optional for doing compassion ministry and justice. It's essential.

But God would not call us to go into all the world and make disciples if it were not possible to do so through His power—and His compassion lived out is an integrated part of that mission. No, His mission is not impossible. But we can't ignore God's provision of power to do it and accomplish it victoriously as He intended.

No, the empowerment of the Holy Spirit is not optional for doing compassion ministry and justice. It's essential.

SPECIFIC NEEDS FOR THE SPIRIT'S ANOINTING IN COMPASSION MINISTRIES

In observing great Pentecostal pioneers in compassion ministries and serving in compassion ministries personally, certain aspects of Christ-like holistic ministry seem especially dependent on the work of the Holy Spirit through God's children. These are biblically grounded in Paul's teaching on the manifestations of the Spirit in 1 Corinthians 12 and 13, and Romans 8, with specific application to twenty-first-century holistic compassion ministries.

THE SPIRITUAL GIFT OF FAITH

The complex mental, physical, emotional, relational, and spiritual needs of millions in our world are overwhelming and seemingly impossible to meet. The closer we get to real people in great need, the more hopeless their situations can seem. It takes the supernatural work of the Spirit to infuse would-be helpers with unnatural faith (sometimes in a moment!)—to

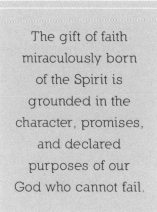

The gift of faith miraculously born of the Spirit is grounded in the character, promises, and declared purposes of our God who cannot fail.

see beyond the visible to what is possible through the Spirit of the Lord. The spiritual gift of faith is not to be confused with a flimsy, naïve, hope-it-all-works-out optimism. The gift of faith miraculously born of the Spirit is grounded in the character, promises, and declared purposes of our God who cannot fail.

> "What no eye has seen, what no ear has heard, and what no human mind has conceived"—the things God has prepared for those who love him—these are the things God has revealed to us by his Spirit. The Spirit searches all things, even the deep things of God.
> (1 Corinthians 2:9–10)

THE SPIRITUAL GIFT OF KNOWLEDGE

The spiritual gift of knowledge demonstrates an awareness of people's lives and needs that are not and could not be known naturally. God works through this spiritual gift to enable His followers to speak with truth into the lives of those in darkness in order to introduce them to the One who is light and salvation. Like the woman at the well who met Jesus (John 4:5–26), people in prisons of disobedience to God play games with truth to make their lives more livable—for themselves and for society. But kindly spoken, spiritually gifted knowledge disarms those in darkness by revealing hidden truth that could only be known supernaturally. This work of the Spirit, articulated through God's anointed children, reveals how much He loves broken prodigal sons and daughters and searches them out for salvation (Luke 19:10). God can work through His children in the spiritual gift of knowledge in refugee camps, slum feeding programs, drug rehab centers, prisons, medical clinics, and brothels—wherever His sons and daughters are compassionately engaged in ministering, and open to the work of His Spirit through them.

THE SPIRITUAL GIFT OF WISDOM

Wisdom is needed if one is to fulfil God's call in challenging spiritual, social, economic, and political contexts. A read through of the life of Christ in the Gospels is enlightening through the lens of God-given wisdom for ministering to people in fluid political and religious environments. Jesus did not fulfill His Father's purposes in a neutral context; and two thousand years later, neither do we. For example, there were times in Jesus' earthly ministry when He told those to whom He ministered, "Go and tell . . ."; yet there were also occasions when He instructed those He had healed not to go and tell what had happened to them. Jesus wisely navigated the political, social, and religious undercurrents in the course of doing His Father's mission. Likewise, as engaged followers of Jesus, we must determine where to go, when to go, when to speak, when to remain silent, what to do, when to do it, how to do it . . . and the list of everyday decisions in fulfilling Christ's mission goes on. In some situations, those decisions can have serious, even life-threatening, consequences. And what "worked" last year (even last week) on the front lines of battle in compassion ministries may not work this year (or week). In a world that is troubled, needy, volatile, and sometimes hostile to Christianity, we can do the will of our Father courageously with quiet confidence. But we must remain healthily dependent on the supernatural gift of wisdom borne of the Spirit to do so.

THE SPIRITUAL GIFT OF DISCERNMENT OF SPIRITS

This spiritual gift is critical if one is to differentiate the needs and underlying spiritual dynamics at work in those we seek to help. The things that I have observed over the past twenty years, as God has guided us into integrated ministry to victims of exploitation and injustice, lead me to suggest strongly that the spiritual gift of discernment is one of the most desperately needed by the missional church today. Yet it is also possibly the most overlooked and least valued.

Perhaps we are reacting in American Pentecostalism to experiences of extreme practices, in which everything was attributed to demons and devils. Today, however, we minister in a different spiritual environment where almost nothing is recognized as being influenced by demonic or satanic power. Instead, erratic behavior or manifestations are attributed to mental illness, emotional instability, or alcoholism. We've gone from assuming a spiritual cause to assuming a natural cause. May God give us the spiritual gift of discernment to rightly discern the needs of those whom we face, because the results of "missing it" can be disheartening at the least, if not destructive and disastrous.

There is one particular phenomenon related to the need for spiritual discernment that I have observed repeatedly in thirty-seven years of ministering with my husband to many young women in youth camps, conferences, and women's events. On a number of occasions during times of prayer and a strong move of God's Spirit, young people would come to us with sincere concern and ask us to pray for someone whom they believed to be "demon-possessed." We would find a group of fervent young people praying—loudly storming heaven!—around a young woman who appeared to be troubled, resistant, and/or out of touch with what was going on around her. It's become David's and my pattern in such situations to ask everyone to move away quietly, continuing to be prayerful, but leaving us alone with the young woman for a few minutes.

When we are still, quiet, and prayerful, it is easier to discern what is happening spiritually in front of us. It's also more sensitive to those for whom we pray. As we quietly pray in Jesus' name, if indeed the powers of darkness and evil are in control, there will be a violent reaction to the presence

> The spiritual gift of discernment is one of the most desperately needed by the missional church today.

and authority of Jesus. The presence of the satanic is personally threatening, not only to the one being prayed for, but also to anyone who tries to intervene in Jesus' name. Prayer of deliverance is needed.

If the person receiving prayer has other deep psychological, emotional, and spiritual needs, when all is still there will be no tangible sense of aggressive evil and the intimidation that comes from our destructive spiritual Enemy. We have noted that although observers may consider a person who was resistant to prayer and responding differently than usual to be under the influence of the demonic, we sometimes privately learn that she has been the victim of sexual abuse in some form. As a result, something in her pulls away from the intense prayer, laying on of hands, and the presence of a holy God when she feels dirty and unworthy. But she is not necessarily controlled by demonic power. Sexual abuse and exploitation definitely seem to open the door for the influence of darkness in the individual violated to varying degrees. It is not infrequent for victims of extreme sexual violence, over time, to become dissociative (formerly called "multiple personality disorder") in order to cope with what is happening to them. They may have fragmented into different personalities, which can be disconcerting, but is not threatening to others. Healing and wise counseling, coupled with spiritual sensitivity, are needed. Victims need Jesus.[75]

In other cases of sexual exploitation, pagan, religious or satanic rituals may have been performed over the woman or child as part of their initiation into prostitution. Sometimes in that process, priests or shamans invite specific gods or goddesses to inhabit the new slave. And the powers of darkness come with a vengeance to trouble her or him for a lifetime unless there is a miraculous deliverance through the greater authority of Jesus and His liberating Spirit.

Hence our desperate need for the spiritual gift of discernment when working with the broken and victimized in compassion ministries. If we are dealing with demonism, we need God's powerful anointing and spiritual authority to pray Spirit-inspired prayers of deliverance. Those delivered can be miraculously set free to love God, serve Him, and live a new life of freedom. But if those we encounter are emotionally and psychologically wounded people, the last thing they need is for followers of Jesus (however well-intentioned) to be praying "demons" out of them and creating more layers of confusion, hurt, and shame. We need the spiritual gift of discernment![76]

THE SPIRITUAL GIFT OF SPIRIT-EMPOWERED PRAYER

In Romans 8:26–27, Paul instructs believers in Spirit-empowered, Spirit-articulated prayer:

---

75 The work and teaching of Dr. Melody Palm, a long-term counselor of victims of sexual abuse internationally, has been invaluable for our understanding and practice. See "Understanding the Psychological Needs of Survivors," *Hands That Heal*, 183.

76 Doug Lowenberg goes into an excellent, theologically sound explanation of the influence of Satan and demonic power in people's lives and the need for believers to discern correctly in order to help. See *Enrichment*, Summer 2013, 93–95.

In the same way, the Spirit helps us in our weaknesses. We do not know what we ought to pray for, but the Spirit Himself intercedes for us through wordless groans. And He who searches our hearts knows the mind of the Spirit, because the Spirit intercedes for God's people in accordance with the will of God.

Similarly, in his letter to the Ephesian believers, Paul exhorts on how to do spiritual battle against the powers of darkness. He describes the essential armor of God and admonishes the Ephesians to practice a life of continual prayer: "Take the helmet of salvation and the sword of the Spirit, which is the word of God. And pray in the Spirit on all occasions with all kinds of prayers and requests . . ." (Eph. 6:17–18).

> And in His sovereign plan, He has chosen to pray by His Spirit through earthen vessels like us to bring desperately needy people to His redemption, healing, and deliverance.

So many times when ministering to those in great need, I am at a loss for words. Humanly speaking, the complexity of human need that is so real, so personal, and so close leaves me fumbling for both wisdom and speech. We are not the answer, and we do not have the answers. But God is, and God does. And in His sovereign plan, He has chosen to pray by His Spirit through earthen vessels like us to bring desperately needy people to His redemption, healing, and deliverance. How privileged we are to participate humbly in His strategy of prayer.

PEOPLE OF THE SPIRIT IN
UNEXPECTED PLACES

One of the greatest joys David and I have experienced in our past decade of ministry has been to meet great men and women of God who are full of His Spirit and walking in Spirit empowerment while doing integrated compassion ministry. I think God has been smiling patiently at us when we've been surprised to learn how much the wind of His Spirit blows across denominational and organizational lines in our world. We've discovered wonderful brothers and sisters of the Spirit doing compassion ministries under all kinds of faith community banners: Baptist, Mennonite, Catholic, Presbyterian, Wesleyan Methodist, Episcopal, nondenominational, World Relief, Pentecostal, Charismatic, Salvation Army, and independent.

As we've gained friends and colleagues across the faith community, we've learned that for many of us the realities of the formidable spiritual battles in the trenches of compassion ministries have forced us to seek God's power and spiritual anointing in greater ways than ever before. With experience, we've learned that our human gifts and strengths are not sufficient for the spiritual battle that is inevitably a part of injustice—even for feeding the hungry. No, fulfilling God's compassionate call needn't lessen our realization that people need evangelism and discipleship as well as food and freedom. It can make us more aware than ever that men, women, boys, and girls need everything God has promised— salvation, discipleship, healing, and deliverance. And so do we. All God's promises for effective integrated mission become possible through the miraculous infilling, power, and gifts of the Holy Spirit at work in His children.

SPIRITUAL AUTHORITY: RECOGNIZING OUR
CULTURAL HANDICAP

One of the most inspiring joys of my spiritual journey has been to watch women of God who had formerly been madams in brothels exercise their God-given spiritual authority over powers of darkness. Women who were formerly tormented by evil spirits and feared their evil power now cast out demons themselves in prayers of deliverance for other enslaved women in a red-light district church. Nothing captures the Great Commission in practice and God's delegated power to accomplish it more than this. It provides a meaningful context for Jesus' last words to His disciples before His ascension into heaven:

> Then Jesus came to them and said, "All authority in heaven and on earth has been given to me. Therefore go and make disciples of all nations, baptizing them in the name of the Father and of the Son and of the Holy Spirit, and teaching them to obey everything I have commanded you. And surely I am with you always, to the very end of the age."
> (Matthew 28:18–20)

As I've observed how quickly former madams in India have assumed and learned to act in their delegated God-given spiritual authority, I've had a growing realization. Madams in brothels understand authority in ways I do not! And madams in brothels in strongly hierarchical cultures understand authority and its delegation especially well. In more hierarchical cultures, the fact that some people have authority is understood, accepted, assumed, and generally unquestioned—whether the authority is ultimately used for good or evil.

What a contrast to those of us who live in more egalitarian cultures where we've been taught it is acceptable—even admired—to question anything and everyone, especially those in authority. So kindergarteners can question their teachers, and egalitarian parents who themselves question authority applaud and support their child's right to question authority. When we've been taught to question authority from birth, should it really be a surprise that we don't easily grasp the meaning of Christ's authority and His delegation of it to us, His followers?

This cultural perspective on authority is an undeniable filter when reading Jesus' words to His first disciples and to us.

> When Jesus had called the Twelve together, he gave them power and authority to drive out all demons and to cure diseases, and he sent them out to proclaim the kingdom of God and to heal the sick.
> (Luke 9:1–2)

> I have given you authority to trample on snakes and scorpions and to overcome all the power of the enemy; nothing will harm you. However, do not rejoice that the spirits submit to you, but rejoice that your names are written in heaven.
> (Luke 10:19–20)

Jesus' words imply that spiritual authority for His disciples is a given, not the big deal. (It is a big deal for those of us who struggle to understand it, receive it, and act on it.) But, rather, Jesus instructs

His disciples to celebrate their salvation based on their relationship to Him. The miracles and spiritual authority over the Evil One flow out of that relationship and are secondary to it. Jesus announced delegated spiritual authority for His disciples. It's not the most important thing; but He assumes we will walk in His authority to fulfill all He has called us to do.

Charles Kraft summarizes, "The authority we participate in is that modeled by Jesus Himself and grounded, as it was with Jesus, in the same power of the Holy Spirit. It is the God-given right to receive and use God's power that flows from the indwelling Holy Spirit."[77]

> Father, transform our minds sadly conformed to culture
> and fill our hungry hearts with your Spirit. We honor your
> authority, we embrace it in our lives, and by your power,
> we will walk in it as we touch others for your glory! Amen.

CONCLUSION

When God's people spend much of our time inside the walls of the church, within youth group, small groups, Bible studies, services, and with other believers, we can be deluded into thinking the infilling of the Holy Spirit promised by Jesus to His disciples in Acts 1:8 is optional: "But you will receive power when the Holy Spirit comes on you; and you will be my witnesses in Jerusalem, and in all Judea and Samaria, and to the ends of the earth." From the comfortable safety of our churches and possibly our work, we can spend minimal time with the addicted, prostituted, broken,

---

77 Charles Kraft, *I Give You Authority: Practicing the Authority Jesus Gave Us* (Grand Rapids, MI: Chosen Books, 2007), 67.

dysfunctional, and exploited. We can comfortably discuss the finer points of our theologies on the Holy Spirit and His work in and through His children, uninterrupted by uncomfortable realities. We might even conclude that the baptism of the Holy Spirit promised believers by Jesus for changing their world is optional and that it's not for us. The task can seem doable talking among ourselves in the community of light.

> On the front line in the epic spiritual battle where darkness and light collide, there is always violent spiritual warfare.

But when we initiate serious steps into the spiritual darkness to take Christ to those in our Isaiah 59 cities and world, delusions of adequacy crumble quickly. Compassion, good intentions, and even faith are not enough. On the front line in the epic spiritual battle where darkness and light collide, there is always violent spiritual warfare. The most courageously engaged followers of Jesus in our world today are desperate for the anointing of the Holy Spirit, and they know it. For the poor, the captive, the slave, the diseased, the victimized, the exploited, and for all sinners like you and me, full freedom only comes through the all-powerful liberating work of the Spirit.

SUGGESTED LEARNING EXPERIENCE

Discuss the following to explore and apply the most pertinent concepts in the chapter.

1. Thinking of men and women of God you know, identify several who live and walk with a recognized spiritual authority in the Spirit. What is it that sets them apart? How do you know, and what does that look like? Share what can be learned from them as spiritual role models for your own life.

2. How does your culture view authority and hierarchy? In what ways personally does that affect or hinder your perspective on Jesus' words and example relative to delegated spiritual authority? Pray together for the Spirit of God to both enlighten and liberate you in the areas of spiritual conformity to culture that is in conflict with God's Word and to work through you.

3. Revisit the apostle Paul's description of the gifts of the Spirit in 1 Corinthians 12. How has God used you as you have been sensitive to His Spirit? Prayerfully identify areas where you are weakest and most desperate for the work of His Spirit in you to fulfill His compassionate purposes among those in spiritual darkness. Pray together for the infilling or renewal of the baptism of the Holy Spirit for empowerment for service.

4. Commit together to seek God intentionally, and to pursue the Holy Spirit's full work personally and corporately for your faith community. Recognize your need for His empowerment in His way. His presence on us and in us is not necessarily loud or demonstrative, but it is unmistakable.

FOR FURTHER READING

- Kendall, R. T. *The Anointing: Yesterday, Today, Tomorrow*. Lake Mary, FL: Charisma House, 2003.

- Kraft, Charles H. *I Give You Authority: Practicing the Authority Jesus Gave Us*. Grand Rapids, MI: Chosen Books, 2007.

- Lowenberg, Doug. "Demonization and the Christian Life: How the Devil Influences Believers." *Enrichment*, Summer 2013, 87–95.

- Menzies, Robert. *Pentecost: This Story Is Our Story*. Springfield, MO: Gospel Publishing House, 2013.

- Tyra, Gary. *The Holy Spirit in Mission: Prophetic Speech and Action in Christian Witness*. Downers Grove, IL: InterVarsity Press, 2011.

CONCLUSION

STANDING UP TO INJUSTICE GOD'S WAY

Biblical justice, like salvation, comes at a cost. Walking the road of discipleship, of justice, demands more than cheap grace. The Bible's basic metaphor for what God is doing in our world is redemption, buying the freedom of someone enslaved. Since we don't live in a slavery society, we tend to miss that meaning. Redemption is a costly transaction.[78]

There is a need in our world and in the lives of followers of Jesus for random acts of kindness. But they are not substitutes for Jesus-centered, courageous compassion and justice that are life-changing and eternity-altering. As the Mother Teresas, Mark and Huldah Buntains, and K. K. Devarajes of our world could attest, it doesn't come easy. Freedom, justice, healing, and transformation are in reality won in the crucible of the epic battle between good and evil, darkness and light. Those who fight the battle with God's eternal truth, in God's way, and with God's empowerment of the Holy Spirit ultimately win great victories in their own lives and on behalf of the lives they seek to redeem.

The most compelling reasons for tackling this book have been two strong currents my husband, David, and I have observed in the past several years. One is the growing tsunami of passion for social justice we observe in a younger generation of followers of Jesus. This is good and right, because our God is a God of justice, and many of us have ignored this strong theme of Scripture for too long.

---

78 David Neff, "Signs of the End Times," *Christianity Today* 55, no. 8 (August 24, 2011): 46–51.

> If we unwittingly separate God's compassionate mission from His spoken truth and liberating Spirit-empowerment, justice and compassion cannot be transformational.

Our young friends and colleagues are courageous to act, articulate in speech, and sincerely ready to take on the most pressing needs and social injustices in our Isaiah 59 world. I love them for it! They represent the greatest potential to genuinely challenge the darkness for Christ's sake of any generation in my lifetime.

The second compelling reason for this book is a deep concern woven through these pages that we get it right. If we unwittingly separate God's compassionate mission from His spoken truth and liberating Spirit-empowerment, justice and compassion cannot be transformational. Our best altruistic efforts, detached from God's great mission, are short-term fixes that may be far more gratifying for us as helpers, advocates, and abolitionists than they are actually life-changing for the poor, the exploited, and the enslaved.

Mathew and Suhasini Daniel have been getting it right for over ten years in Pune, India. When they agreed to take eighteen young trafficked girls rescued in government raids into a Project Rescue aftercare home for healing, the task looked formidable. And it *was* formidable, as they had to incorporate every bit of medical expertise, trauma counseling, social work, and spiritual deliverance ministry they could muster to begin to meet the physical, emotional, psychological, educational, and spiritual needs of the girls in their care.

The Daniels have literally fought for the lives of their adopted "daughters"—against landlords who threw them out when they realized the girls' background; against relatives in the red-light districts who fought to get them back for exploitation; against would-be ministry partners who would have re-exploited the traumatized girls in the name of "helping;" against traffickers in court when the girls were ready to tell their stories; and against the violent powers of darkness that took control of too many nights until these beautiful girls experienced total deliverance.

Fourteen of the girls have now finished the aftercare program and graduated from school. They are preparing for vocations and professions as confident, educated young women of God. As this manuscript was being written, seven survivors began a college certificate program in counseling. Their passionate calling is to become caregivers and staff for sexually exploited girls in their nation who, like themselves ten years ago, need freedom, healing, and Jesus. These former victims of child sex-trafficking have themselves become compelling voices for freedom and justice.

Mathew and Suha would be the first to acknowledge they have made mistakes. But they worked hard, prayed harder, and collaborated with others to do compassion and justice with integrity and open loyalty to Jesus while implementing a program that earned the respect of government and social services—no small feat. If followers of Jesus attempt to do compassion and justice in an Isaiah 59 world without introducing the poor, needy, and exploited to Jesus, the liberating truth of God's Word, a supportive community of faith, and the power of the Holy Spirit, the following results are all too common:

- Slaves liberated physically to new safe locations remain slaves in mind and spirit.

- In disheartening numbers, they return to exploitation again.

- The poor who have received financial aid alone will continue to be bound by mental, psychological, social, and spiritual poverty.

- Healing for the sexually exploited will be limited to the best of human counseling and care without the opportunity to experience the miracle of spiritual transformation.

And when rescued girls return to their slavery, the poor continue to be poor, or those we have helped become exploiters themselves, we can become disillusioned, pull back in frustration, and tragically conclude that God's justice doesn't really work after all. Far too many former fighters in this battle have already quietly done so.

Those in the church who have warned against involvement with social justice and compassion will say, "See, focusing on social justice is a distraction from the gospel, from evangelism, from discipleship—from the Great Commission. It's too easy to lose focus on our priorities. Don't go there." The fragmentation of Jesus' whole Luke 4:18 mandate continues with seeming justification. And the poor, exploited, and enslaved lose most.

Lastly, those in bondage resign themselves again to the lie of the Enemy that no one can possibly give them a different future. Promises are cheap. Our best efforts and most valiant work at justice cannot force the hand of God nor humanly transform broken wills to make healthy choices for good after years of trauma and failure. But God's justice does work . . . when we do it God's way. His miraculous mission to redeem the lost, the broken, the diseased, and the captive does work when His children fiercely, faithfully follow His Jesus-centered, Spirit-empowered, community-of-faith building New Testament strategy.

> God's justice does work . . . when we do it God's way.

And on the hardest days in the battle against evil, when we've done all we can do, we call upon His name. God sustains us and miraculously transforms lives of men, women, boys, and girls as He promises—because this is His mission, and we dare to do it His way.

Is not this the kind of fasting I have chosen:
to loose the chains of injustice
and untie the cords of the yoke,
to set the oppressed free
and break every yoke?
Is it not to share your food with the hungry
and to provide the poor wanderer with shelter—
when you see the naked, to clothe them,
and not to turn away from your own flesh and blood?
Then your light will break forth like the dawn,
and your healing will quickly appear;
then your righteousness will go before you,
and the glory of the LORD will be your rear guard.
Then you will call, and the LORD will answer;
you will cry for help, and he will say: Here am I.
(Isaiah 58:6–9)

APPENDICES

Appendix A

PRACTICAL GUIDELINES FOR ASSESSING COMPASSION MINISTRIES FOR PERSONAL OR CORPORATE INVOLVEMENT OR SUPPORT

Before volunteering with or supporting a compassion ministry, it is strategic to ask the following questions:

1. How is the ministry connected to and viewed by the local community? Is it being done to or with the local community? In what ways?

2. Is the ministry in partnership with a local community of faith/church on the ground? If so, how?

3. Is the staff largely local/national or foreign? If foreign, to what extent is there joint ownership with the local community of faith?

4. Is there accountability to local spiritual leadership; if so, how does it function?

5. Are there local structures of ministry in place to take the compassion ministry to individuals beyond meeting physical needs to spiritual transformation, an opportunity for those in need to become "new creations in Christ Jesus"?

6. Describe how the ministry is missional like the compassionate ministry of Jesus?

Appendix B

HOW DOES THE MINISTRY FIT WITH
OUR LARGER AGWM MISSION?

REACHING Evangelism	PLANTING Growing Churches	TRAINING Discipleship	TOUCHING Compassion
Red-light district and street outreach	Planting red-light district churches	In every aftercare home for women and children	Intervention for physical rescue
Medical clinics	Vocational training center (sensitive areas)	In red-light district churches & Sunday Schools	Ensuring education
District Sunday schools and after-school programs	Starting care cell groups in or near areas of prostitution for men and women	In local churches that become faith community for those in programs	Trauma counseling
In aftercare homes		Bible School scholarships for those called to vocational ministry	Medical clinics

Note: Out of eleven Project Rescue affiliated sites in six countries, only one ministry, which has existed for twenty years, has included all these facets: Bombay Teen Challenge in Mumbai, India. Others included their first intervention ministry where God first opened a door, and then grew into these four elements in different forms based on their local cultural, political, and religious contexts. No two ministries look the same, but all are mutually committed to the four elements of the mission.

Appendix C

RECOMMENDED INTERNATIONAL
ORGANIZATION WEBSITES

The following websites are offered for readers who want more information about how to become involved in integrated Jesus-centered compassion ministries and/or initiatives ministering to victims of social injustice, sex trafficking, and sexual exploitation around the world. While there are many good organizations providing excellent services, those below are included for their commitment to providing transformational compassion and justice that address the needs of the whole person—body, mind, and spirit.

Websites for recommended integrated compassion ministries

Convoy of Hope	www.convoyofhope.org
Enlace El Salvador	www.enlaCEOnline.org
Global Teen Challenge	www.globaltc.org
drug/substance abuse rehab	
Health Care Ministries	www.healthcareministries.org
Latin America Child Care	www.lacc4hope.org
Rainbows of Hope and Crisis Care Training International	www.wecinternational.org.uk org.uk/wec-youth-children
global ministries of WEC International	-camps/children-risk-crisis
to children in crisis	-roh.html
Salvation Army	www.salvationarmy.org
Touched Romania	www.touchedromania.org

World Hope   www.worldhope.org

World Relief   www.worldrelief.org

Websites for recommended transformational
ministries specifically working with victims of sexual
exploitation and sex trafficking, or children at high risk

Alabaster Jar   www.alabasterjar.de
Germany

Bombay Teen Challenge   www.bombayteenchallenge.org

Breaking Chains Network   www.breakingchainsnetwork.com
Belgium

Chab Dai Cambodia   wwwmogiv.com/chabdai/cambodia/

Chicas de Promesa   www.marykmahon.com
Costa Rica

Faith Alliance Against   www.faastinternational.org
Slavery and Trafficking

Live2free   www.live2free.org
*US university student
engagement*

Project Rescue   www.projectrescue.com

Project Rescue Spain   www.fietgratia.org

Rescue: Freedom   www.rescuefreedom.org
International

Appendix D

LEARNING EXERCISE FOR CHAPTER 8, COMMUNITY OF DARKNESS, COMMUNITY OF LIGHT

Purpose of activity: to demonstrate the power of community for both good and evil, it's impact on the efforts of people of faith to live out God's justice, and its impact on those in bondage and exploitation whom they seek to help.

Directions: Divide group/class into two seated groups divided by a physical space of at least four to five feet. Identify one group as the community of faith (light) and one as the community of injustice and exploitation (darkness). Identify a person from the community of light who wants to help rescue people from the community of darkness.

Moderator asks each community, "What are the qualities that characterize your community? "Of the community of light, "Are the qualities named generally true or ideal?"

Have rescuer come out of their community to stand in space between the two communities. He or she then brings a young woman out of the community of darkness into the space between the two communities.

As rescuer and rescued stand together between communities, moderator asks the following questions:

1. (To the community of darkness/exploitation) What are you thinking/feeling when this person comes to take this person out of your community? What are your fears? How might you respond? Why?

2. (To the rescuer) Now, you have gotten this person out, what are you going to do with this person?

3. (To the person being rescued) Given where you have been, what might be your thoughts/ feelings/fears? How might you respond? Why?

4. (To the community of light) So this member of your community of light wants to bring this woman/man out of the bondage of the community of darkness. What might be your thoughts, feelings, fears, reactions? Why?

5. What specific thoughts, feelings, and fears may occur if those coming out of darkness have been involved in sexual exploitation as victim or perpetrator? What is our responsibility as followers of Jesus to them? What is the responsibility of pastors and leaders in this kind of situation?

In order to help people find freedom from slavery, exploitation, and injustice, those who engage must be prepared to bring them into a local, supportive healing community. Without that, they cannot usually survive alone, and end up pulled back into their old community of exploitation.

Discuss the following:

1. Propose some practical steps you could take to prepare your local community of faith to be the kind of biblical New Testament community where healing, life-changing journeys can occur?

2. What spiritual issues and cultural attitudes would need to be addressed? How?

3. Is it responsible to try and "rescue" the poor, enslaved, and exploited if the local community of faith is not yet prepared to receive them in grace, faith, and patience for the messy journey of healing? Why or why not?

4. What is the most important insight into your community of faith, the community of darkness, or yourself personally that you have gained through the exercise?

Concluding prayer: Pray for God to reveal and forgive personal attitudes, thoughts, and motives about those in the community of light or darkness that are not pleasing to God. Pray for God's wisdom to know how to engage injustice locally and practice Jesus' compassion with integrity as a community.

Pray for the Spirit's transformation of attitudes and perspectives to more clearly reflect the image of Jesus.

Pray for growing faith, unity, and Spirit-empowerment to fulfill Jesus' Luke 4:18 mandate and mission.

ABOUT THE AUTHOR

Beth Grant and her husband, David, have served as Assemblies of God ministers to Eurasia for thirty-seven years. While their ministry has focused on the land of India, their heart for international ministry has carried them to over thirty nations of the world.

Beth's calling and passion is that of teacher. She serves as faculty and guest lecturer in international ministry and intercultural education in colleges in India, Asia, Africa, Europe, and the United States. She speaks frequently at women's retreats internationally, inspiring women to recognize their identity in Christ and be empowered to fulfill their God-given purpose.

Beth serves as codirector of Project Rescue, a ministry to survivors of sexual slavery. As a member of the Faith Alliance Against Slavery and Trafficking, Beth coedited *Hands That Heal*, an international curriculum to train caregivers of trafficking survivors. She currently serves as the first female executive presbyter with The General Council of the Assemblies of God USA.

Beth completed a PhD in Intercultural Education from Biola University in Los Angeles, California. Her vision is to mobilize a generation of young women and men to fulfill God's transforming mission in our twenty-first-century world.

Beth's most valued roles are that of wife to David, mother to two wonderful daughters, Rebecca and Jennifer, mother-in-law to Tyler Shults and Jon Barratt, and "Mimi" to Judah and Gemma.